Pizza Napoletana!

Pizza Napoletana!

TEXT & RECIPES BY PAMELA SHELDON JOHNS

PRODUCED BY JENNIFER BARRY DESIGN

PHOTOGRAPHY BY RICHARD G. JUNG

TEN SPEED PRESS

BERKELEY, CALIFORNIA

A Kirsty Melville Book

Ten Speed Press
Box 7123, Berkeley, California 94707
www.tenspeed.com

Distributed in Australia by Simon & Schuster Australia, in Canada by Ten Speed Press Canada,
in New Zealand by Southern Publishing Group, in South Africa by Real Books, in Southeast Asia
by Berkeley Books, and in the United Kingdom and Europe by Airlift Books.

Concept and Design: Jennifer Barry Design, Sausalito, California
Production Assistant: Kristen Wurz
Copy Editor: Carolyn Miller
Food Stylist: Pouké
Prop Stylist: Carol Hacker/Tableprop

Library of Congress Cataloging-in-Publication Data
Johns, Pamela Sheldon
Pizza Napoletana! / text and recipes by Pamela Sheldon Johns;
produced by Jennifer Barry Design; photography by Richard Jung.
p.   cm.
"A Kirsty Melville book"--T.p. verso.
Includes bibliographical references.
ISBN 1-58008-085-5
1. Pizza. 2. Pizza--Italy--Naples. I. Title.
TX770.P58J64   1999
641.8'24--dc21   99-14301
CIP

Printed in Singapore
First printing, 1999
1 2 3 4 5 6 7 8 9 10 — 03 02 01 00 99

Contents

Introduction

Whipping in and out of the narrow alleys of Naples, weaving through traffic that blared a cacophony of sounds, going down one-way streets the wrong way and against red lights, and amid the somewhat, and thankfully, incomprehensible words of the taxi driver slung out the window to his driving adversaries, I mustered the courage and vocabulary to ask, "*Qual' é la tua pizza preferita?* (What is your favorite pizza?)" He turned his head towards me, and away from the road a little too long for comfort, and simply said, "*Margherita.*"

Pizza is one of the world's most popular versions of flat bread. Every culture has an interpretation of a hearth-baked grain dough, from the tortillas of the Americas to Armenian lavosh. Flat bread is one of the most ancient cooked foods—evidence of these breads has been found at prehistoric sites. A source of vital energy, eaten by even the poorest people, this mixture of crushed grains and water could be cooked using only a

stone and fire. In Italy, flat bread evolved into many unique regional forms, still found in today's bakeries: Romagna's *piadina*, for one, and Tuscany's Etruscan-era *schiacciata*, now called focaccia throughout the country. Focaccia literally means "flat bread," from the Latin root, *focacius*, meaning "hearth." These breads were once considered peasant food and were sold on the streets to those too poor to have their own ovens.

When the tomato made its way from the Americas through Spain to Italy in the late 1700s, it was Naples, in the southern region of Campania, that found a place for it on its flat breads. Now pizza is the single most popular food item attributed to Italy. Italian culinary expert Carol Field calls pizza the "first national dish of the country."

Naples, the victim and benefactor of many conquests, has a deep and rich history. Founded by the Greeks and called Neapolis, it was a central part of the Magna Graecia realm. The Romans lived here in the fourth century B.C.,

~

All over southern
Italy, you see bright
red cherry tomatoes
hanging in clusters
from the rafters of
the kitchens. These are
called pomodorini
del piennolo, and are the
approved DOC tomatoes
to slice and serve on the
Margherita Extra.

~

and the Spanish and the French, among others, have all left their marks on the language, architecture, and cuisine. Neapolitans lay claim to the birthplace of pizza, though history would give more credit to the Greeks and Romans. The author Elizabeth Romer describes the modern Neapolitan passion for pizza as a cult in Naples. It is an apt description, for in Naples, mythology, passion, and pizza entwine.

Naples was at its height in the 1780s, full of Bourbon wealth and spirit. Street vendors bought pizzas from small stands and roamed the city selling slices from a lidded metal box or a *tavolino*, a narrow board. The stands made pizza to order

with simple, seasonal ingredients, including the newly discovered tomato. It was probably at this time that pizza marinara, with its topping of tomatoes, garlic, oregano, and olive oil, was born. A pizza delivered to King Ferdinando I and Queen Maria Carolina from Taverna del Cerriglio was said to be so well received that the king had a red-tiled pizza oven built at the Capodimonte Palace. (Another version of the story is that Maria Carolina, a Hapsburg princess, wouldn't allow pizza in the palace, so the king had

to go out for his favorite food. Tiring of the inconvenience, he built his own oven.)

In 1830, **Antica Pizzeria Port'Alba**, the first *pizzeria*, opened in the heart of Naples. It quickly became a meeting place for the man in the street. For those who could afford it, there were pizzas topped with fresh shellfish and seafood, buffalo mozzarella, cured meats, and sometimes *cecinielli*, tiny white fish that are still in the larval stage of development. One popular pizza that no longer exists, the *Mastunicola*, was topped with lard, grated pecorino (sheep's milk) cheese, and basil. Oregano and basil were the favored herbs, as today. But because so many of the patrons were artists, students, or workers living on a shoestring, the most common pizza was seasoned simply with oil and garlic. The *pizzerie* developed a system for payment called *pizza a otto*: eat now, pay eight days later. The local joke became the question of whether pizza might be a man's last free meal—if he died before he paid. Pizza was sold to passersby, along with deep-fried bits of dough studded with prosciutto, herbs, or pieces of cheese and shaped into a variety of forms that were easy to carry and eat. These were originally made from odds and ends of dough, but eventually evolved into a new form, fried pizza, which can still be found in some *pizzerie.*

"*Qual' é la tua pizza preferita?*" I asked the gentleman sitting next to me, "What pizza do you like best?" This taxi driver certainly impressed me as a gentleman, suit and tie, car neat as a pin, opera playing on the radio. Without hesitation, he answered, "*La mia preferita é la pizza Margherita,*" and spent the rest of our ride telling me the history of its name and his favorite *pizzerie.*

As the story goes, the first classic pizza Margherita was made, or at least named, by Raffaele Esposito of Pietro il Pizzaiolo *pizzeria,* now called **Pizzeria Brandi**. In 1889, Esposito was invited to the palace to create three pizzas for the visit of King Umberto and Queen Margherita of Savoy. The queen declared that her favorite was the patriotic one resembling the Italian flag with its colors of red (tomatoes), white (mozzarella cheese), and green (basil). The pizza quickly became one of the classic pizzas of Naples and has been called "Pizza Margherita," after the queen, to this day.

In the late 1800s, life was extremely hard for Italian peasants. At the turn of the century, five million made their way to America, 80 percent of them from the south. Their culture and cuisine accompanied them to the Americas: The first *pizzeria* in New York was opened by Neapolitan Gennaro Lombardi in 1905 (originally at 53 Spring Street, now reopened at 32 Spring Street). Today pizza is a thirty-billion-dollar industry. In pizza's migrations, the crust has thinned and thickened, the shape has taken many forms, and the toppings have stretched the imagination to its limits. Culinary expert Burton Anderson calls American pizza "born again," because of the changes in size, form, baking methods, and ingredients it has undergone.

It has only been in the last twenty years or so that *pizzerie* in Naples evolved into sit-down dining establishments. Now, even the finest restaurants may have a wood-burning oven to offer pizza as a first course. And, conversely, some *pizzerie* have begun to add other courses to their menus. The colorful streets of Naples are still sprinkled with little stands selling pizza by the slice, *a libretto,* folded in half "like a book."

~

Historically,
the local cheeses used
for pizza included
mozzarella made with the
milk of water buffalo,
provolone and caciocavallo
made with cow's milk,
and sheep's milk pecorino.
Today, many cheeses are
imported from other regions
and have been accepted
in the kitchens of Naples,
especially Gorgonzola,
Parmigiano-Reggiano,
and fontina.

~

Pizza has made its way throughout the entire country of Italy. In the fifties and sixties, as families moved to the industrialized north seeking work, they brought with them their favorite food. Indeed, in Italy the total sales of *pizzerie* exceed the sales of Fiat, the country's largest car company. Local pizzas have become as accepted as the other indigenous foods of the area, incorporating unique regional ingredients and variations to produce a new tradition.

There must be thousands of interpretations of pizza. Few developed countries are without pizza, and every culture has made its own stamp. You can find pizza in Japan topped with lotus root. There are pizza chain restaurants in Moscow. In spite of all of these diversions, in Naples there lives a true patriotism for the original pizza. Many believe that the best pizza is found here. In the next pages, we will explore the precise methods and ingredients needed to re-create the true, original pizza of Naples, then explore regional variations, along with some other popular hearth breads and similar dough preparations. But first we must start with the two most classic pizzas from Naples: the Margherita, topped with tomatoes, buffalo mozzarella, olive oil, and fresh basil, and the marinara, topped with tomatoes, olive oil, garlic, and oregano.

Pizza Napoletana

With a production of an estimated seven million pizzas a day in Italy and so many wild interpretations burgeoning all over the world, it is no wonder that a group of local *pizzaioli*, or pizza makers, decided to join together in the mid-nineties to create an organization, Associazione Vera Pizza Napoletana, to defend the integrity of their product. The association has even instituted courses resulting in a diploma. Their logo is an image of the popular Neapolitan character Pulcinella ("Punch") holding a pizza paddle. Display of the emblem indicates that a *pizzeria* serves *vera pizza napoletana*, or true Neapolitan pizza. The standards are based on the work of Carlo Mangoni, professor of physiology and nutrition at the Second University of Naples.

In alliance with the city of Naples, Professor Mangoni

was asked to provide research to establish the traditional ingredients and methods used to make a true Neapolitan pizza. The result was a forty-two-page document that outlined the historical roots of pizza, explored the traditional ingredients and the precise preparation and cooking process, and concluded with a detailed nutritional analysis.

This report was the first step in attempting to establish a DOC for pizza, a designation that can be compared to wine-making DOC zones. The Denominazione di Origine Controllata (denomination of controlled origin) not only determines the geographic origin of specific foods and wines, but also outlines permitted ingredients and defines the production process. Leading the way again, Professor Mangoni prepared the documents necessary to request approval from Ente Nazionale Italiano di Unificazione (UNI), the governmental agency designated to establish the laws and regulation of arts, goods, and services in Italy.

The approval process began with interviews of forty Neapolitan pizza makers who had been asked to explain their pizza-making practices. The university labs then tested and completely analyzed the dough, the tomatoes, and the oil. Studies included such intricate work as stage-by-stage microscopic photos of the dough rising. A detailed explanation of this work is found in the following chapter.

In June 1998, the good news arrived: Authentic *pizza napoletana, verace pizza napoletana,* had become a protected entity. The legal designation is limited to two pizzas: Margherita and marinara. Mayor Antonio Bassolino revealed the new logo at a grand ceremony: a brilliant primary blue background "like the sky of Naples," the outline of Mt. Vesuvius in bold white strokes, and in the foreground, an abstract rendition of the pizza Margherita, with the red of the tomato and white rounds of buffalo mozzarella. Two leaves of basil form the letter V in the word *verace,* authentic, and also dot the "i" of the word "Pizza." This regulating mark for *pizza napoletana*, like the black rooster of Chianti, is granted to those who guarantee the acceptance of the regulations set forth and are willing to subject their work to review.

Nothing in the regulations says that the pizza must be made in Naples, much less Italy. Any restaurant in the world can make the guarantee that their production of the two pizzas meets the requirements of the DOC. Mayor Bassolino says, "In a sense, this initiative is our consent to export to the world our gastronomic culture by standardizing the rules and guaranteeing good dining, and in return we welcome the visitor back to its home. We will be able to make known to the world the quality of our products." Bassolino's first project was to launch an annual Pizzafest in the first week of October, modeled after Germany's Oktoberfest.

Even in Naples, in most *pizzerie*, you must ask for "pizza DOC." If you simply order Margherita or marinara, you may get a variation that uses *fior di latte*, cow's milk mozzarella, instead of *mozzarella di bufala* (see detailed explanation on page 37), or instead of a garnish of olive oil, seed oil may be used.

Even with the specific delineation of the DOC, some variation in interpretations will surely remain, for the *pizzaiolo* is an artisan. Come along with me for a quick visit to some of my favorite *pizzerie* to discover what constitutes the true Neapolitan pizza.

Making and Shaping the Dough

I've wandered my way through narrow *vicoli*, alleys brimming with shops displaying breads and cheeses alongside stands of sumptuous produce displays of garlic garlands and *pomodorini del piennolo*, hanging bunches of cherry tomatoes. I've passed through the grand openness of Naples's main piazza, Piazza del Plebiscito, cobbled and spacious. Near here is the Teatro San Carlo, Italy's largest opera house; the palace; and the impressive galleria of gilt and glass.

There is a very different feeling to this part of Naples.

I can't help myself as I stop to ask a policeman for directions to Via Alabardieri: "*Qual'é la tua pizza preferita?*" I wasn't surprised to hear the answer: Margherita.

Massimo di Porzio has worked at **Umberto**, his family restaurant/*pizzeria*, since he was twelve years old. His grandfather, Umberto, opened the place as a little trattoria in 1921. Don Umberto was known for his selection of exceptional local wines and excellent food. Banking on this reputation, he enlarged in 1926. "A restaurant isn't made only by its customers," he was known to say. "It is the use of authentic ingredients that creates its reputation." Leopoldo Arienzo, the pizza maker at Umberto for more than fifty years, lived by that creed.

"Pizza is the crust," say the Neapolitans. Of all of the components in their product, it is the simple combination of flour, water, salt, and yeast that makes it unique. The secret is in the overall rising time—at least 6 hours or longer. Very little yeast is used for this slow rise, and the result is a dough that is moist and very soft.

According to the DOC stipulations, it is permissible to use an approved mixer to make the dough. Considering the quantity of dough needed on a daily basis, this was a practical recommendation. Even with a mixer, the dough

must knead for 30 minutes, so it is important that the mixer does not overheat the dough and kill the yeast.

Once the dough has risen for the first 4 hours, it is shaped into *pagnotte,* little balls weighing about 6 ounces each. The *pizzaiolo* knows by look and feel how to portion the dough out, and he stretches and tightens each ball firmly

customers thanked me for bringing back the fried pizzas—it made them recall their childhood. I felt the same way. It was something my mother made us for after school."

Stretching the Dough

On the other side of town, right at the edge of the old part

before placing it in a wooden, lidded chest, the *madia,* to rise for another 2 to 4 hours.

Massimo and his siblings, Linda, Lorella, and Roberta, have given Umberto's sunny dining room a youthful vigor, but there is still a respect for tradition. Massimo says, "Many

of Naples, is the ancient city gate of San Gennaro, rebuilt in the mid-fifteenth century after the city walls had been moved. As you pass through it, it is hard not to reflect on the history of this portal, with its recently restored Mattia Preti fresco from the 1600s. Set into the wall is a statue of the Virgin Mary, gilded, beflowered, and protected behind glass. Steps away, on the old stone wall, is an elegant marble plaque stating simply: **Capasso**.

Gaetano Capasso and his uncle Vincenzo are fixtures at Capasso. This tiny restaurant offers a full range of antipasti; *primi piatti*, or first courses; and meat and fish main courses; but there is no mistaking what the focal point is. Vincenzo is the quiet king of his pizza oven, the preeminent sight as you enter, its open door glowing a welcome.

Vincenzo keeps the rising dough in the *madia* until he is ready to make a pizza. The dough is not disturbed until the pizza is ordered. *Pizzaioli* in Naples do not toss the dough in the air. Perhaps because it is such a soft and pliable dough, it is patted out on a lightly floured work table. And according to the DOC regulations, this process may not be done with a machine, only by hand. The *pagnotte* are patted flat from the center out with the fingertips, leaving the rim slightly puffy to create the *cornicione*, the outer edge of crust that puffs up. Additional stretching

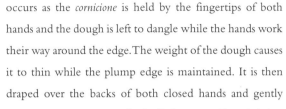

occurs as the *cornicione* is held by the fingertips of both hands and the dough is left to dangle while the hands work their way around the edge. The weight of the dough causes it to thin while the plump edge is maintained. It is then draped over the backs of both closed hands and gently stretched a little more. When it is just the right size, it is placed on the work table ready to be assembled.

Assembling the Pizza

Everything about **Trianon da Ciro** seems large, even the imposing stature of its fourth-generation owner, Ciro Leone. From the second level, the restaurant overlooks the teeming streets of Naples; inside it is a panorama of marble, with seating for over four hundred. Even the pizzas are big. Their specialty is the *ruota di carretto*, a giant pizza topped with your choice of seasonal ingredients. Though they offer DOC pizza, my favorite was topped with sausages and sautéed *friarielli*, a bitter green found only in Campania. The fresh green resembles broccoli rabe, but it is part of the cabbage family. Each mouthful is richly packed with

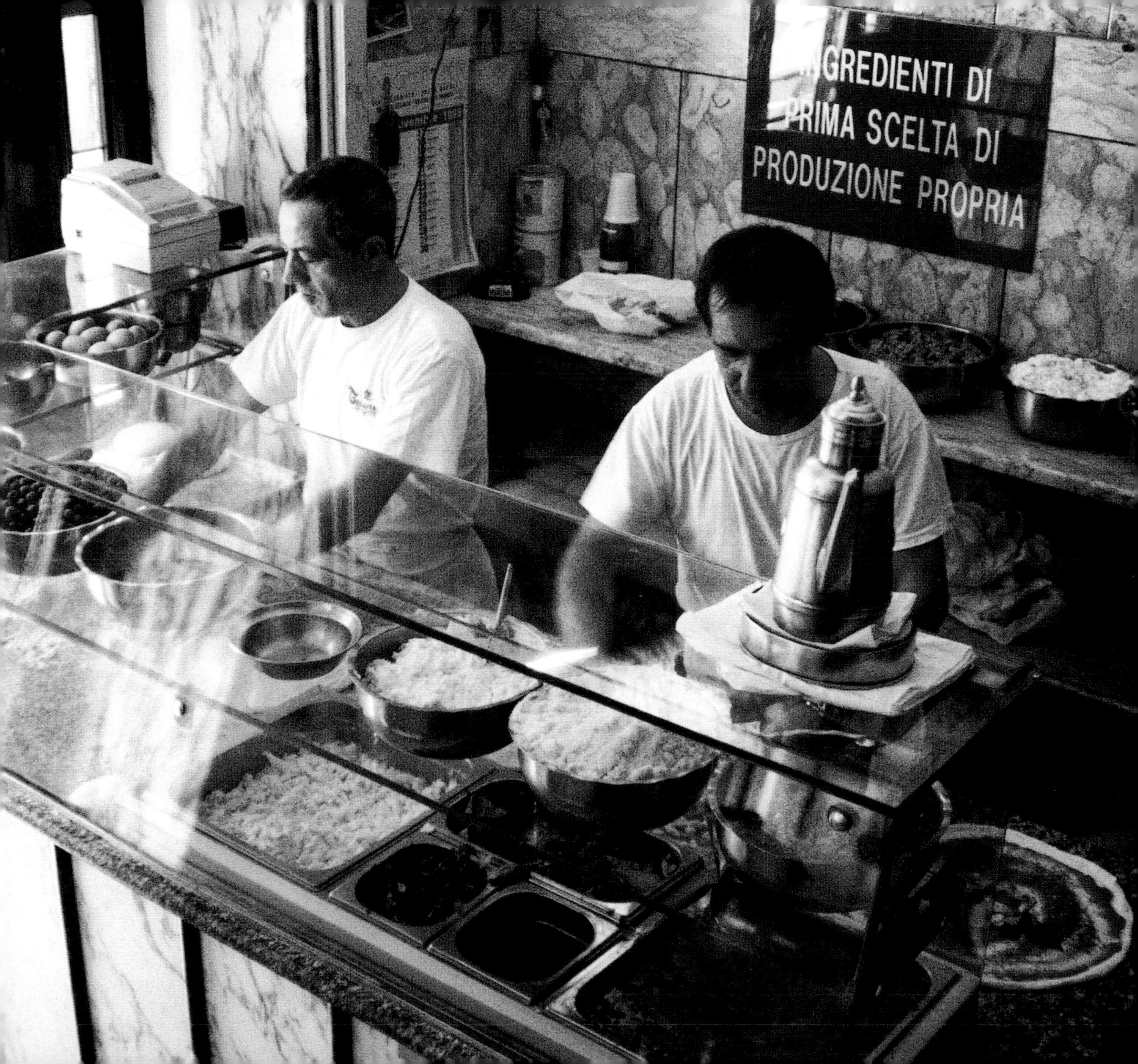
INGREDIENTI DI
PRIMA SCELTA DI
PRODUZIONE PROPRIA

minerals and vitamins; it reminded me of *cavolo nero*, the black cabbage of Tuscany. The local sausage is made with pork, veal, peperoncini, and garlic, marinated in wine, and smoked over fires of green poplar wood. These big flavors match the size of Trianon.

A restaurant this large is a study in efficiency. Of the three pizza ovens, the main one greets you as you enter the casual *pizzeria* on the ground level. In the glass-fronted marble case, the *pagnotte* stand ready to be stretched. All of the essential toppings have been prepared and organized for a quick assembly.

Neapolitan pizzas are scantily dressed. The stretched rounds of dough are assembled on the flour-dusted marble next to the toppings. Crushed fresh San Marzano tomatoes are swirled from the center for the Margherita; slices of mozzarella, a few leaves of basil, and a sprinkle of salt are added. All of the ingredients used are raw, as the temperature of the pizza oven is high and the cooking time is quick.

The final touch is a drizzle of oil from the *agliara*,

dialect for the brass oil can found on every pizza maker's marble counter. Although the true *pizza napoletana* is finished with olive oil, in most *pizzerie* the *agliara* is filled with seed oil. Less than 2 minutes later, it is out of the oven, garnished with a couple of fresh basil leaves, and sped at once to the table.

Variations on Ingredients

According to the DOC document, there are only two true Neapolitan pizzas. However, a couple of variations are allowed for the Margherita. The first, called *Margherita classica*, allows the addition of grated cheese, specifically Parmigiano-Reggiano, pecorino, or grana padano. The second variation, *Margherita Extra*, adds sliced fresh tomato. Beyond the DOC pizzas, most *pizzerie* offer a large variety of toppings to choose from, but those who serve DOC *pizze* don't usually stray too far from home. There are several other quasi-classic pizzas found in the pizzerie of Naples. One such pizza is the *quattro stagione*, or four seasons pizza. The round is divided into quadrants, each with a different ingredient.

The wood-burning oven is an icon of the suppressed heat and cool exterior of Mt. Vesuvius, the only active volcano in continental Europe. Neapolitans savor each moment of their lives fully, as if to experience as much as possible in the event of another eruption.

One of the specialties of **Cantanapoli** is a quattro stagione with as many as eight or sixteen toppings. The choices tend to be seasonal. It is popular to divide each section with a strip of dough. Cantanapoli is a visual sensation. It has a festive atmosphere set against the background of a sea-themed mural. The waiters, in scarlet knickers with scarves tied around their heads, serve elaborate pizzas at banquet-sized tables filled with families. Owner Carmine de Pompeis is in constant motion. "Pavarotti ate here," he says as he seats another group of businessmen.

The Oven

By definition, *pizza napoletana* must be cooked in a wood-burning oven. One of my fondest memories of Italy is sitting in the kitchen of friends and looking into a wood-burning oven at our pizzas puffing and browning. In a Naples *pizzeria*, the fire is almost never out. The oven stays warm with embers until the next kindling. Some, like the one at **Lombardi a Santa Chiara,** look like architectural edifices. All are made of interior bricks formed of clay rich in alumina, a mineral that heats quickly and uniformly. A domed ceiling reduces the

problem of hot and cold spots and promotes heat retention.

Since 1890, Lombardi has been a pizza institution in Spaccanapoli, the heart of Naples. In the early days, many boats stopped in Naples on their way to the Americas. Founder Enrico Lombardi brought a portable oven to the wharf to make fried calzones and pizzas for the travelers. When the boats were not in port, he was a traveling *pizzaiolo*, moving through the narrow streets of Naples. Later, his son Luigi established a stand near the bell tower of the fourteenth-century Santa Chiara church, thereby fixing the name Lombardi a Santa Chiara. Today's *pizzeria* is still in the same neighborhood, near Piazza Gesù Nuovo. Enrico's grandsons, Alfonso and Luigi, continue the tradition, with excellent pizza and other traditional dishes.

Several hours before service, the *pizzaiolo* removes all of the ashes from the last use of the oven. A hardwood fire is lit in the center of the oven. The DOC document specifies that the wood should not smoke or give off an odor that will modify the aroma of the pizza. After a couple of hours, when the flames have died to embers and the roof of the oven has gone from black to whitish gray, the fire is moved to the side of the oven. The correct temperature for pizza is 750° to 800°F.

The *spazzola*, a fireproof brush, is used to sweep the ashes away from the central cooking area. The fire on the periphery is kept alive throughout the night. The temperature can be adjusted by adding more wood or opening the door slightly. Experienced pizza chefs determine the proper temperature by the color of the oven's interior and the rate at which the food is cooking.

Once the pizza is garnished and placed on the wooden paddle, the *pizzaiolo* slides it into the oven to the place he wants it to cook. With a short forward jerk of the wrist, he slides it onto the floor of the oven. A quick pull of the paddle backward completes the maneuver. The experienced *pizzaiolo* knows the hot and cool spots in his oven and watches a pizza carefully, moving it around and turning it slightly with the *palo di infornare*, a pizza paddle with a long handle. In less than 2 minutes, the pizza is ready.

Eating Pizza

Ask several people if pizza should be eaten for lunch or dinner, and you will get different answers. In many parts of Italy, pizza is eaten only at dinner, but in Naples it is available at all times of the day. **Da Michele,** also known as Pizzeria Condurro, opens at eight in the morning and doesn't close until quite late. In this lively quarter near the train station, pizza continues its long tradition as the meal of choice for the workingman. This *pizzeria* has been in its present location since 1930, and not much of its simple interior seems to have changed. The business was started in this same neighborhood in 1900 by Michele and Anna Maria Gargivolo and has passed in the traditional way, from father to son, to today's proprietor, Michele Condurro. His son Marco works with him.

The remarkable thing about Da Michele is that they serve only Margherita and marinara pizzas, and sometimes a calzone version. According to Michele Condurro, 80 percent of the pizzas served are Margherita. On the wall are poems dedicated to the simplicity of the two true

Neapolitan pizzas. They used to serve the pizzas directly on the marble tables, but now plates are used.

For the culmination of our pizza journey, we go across town. No address is needed for this cab driver, just the name, **Ciro a Santa Brigida**. I can't resist one last poll: "*Qual' è la tua pizza preferita?*" I ask him as we race down Corso Vittorio Emanuele. I thought I knew what the response would be, but he declares, "*Senza dubbio, la marinara!*" ("Without a doubt, it's marinara!") Ah, I knew it had to get at least one vote.

Today's meal could be described as the verace pizza power lunch. Hosted by Antonio Pace, owner of Ciro a Santa Brigida and president of Associazione Vera Pizza Napoletana, we are joined by professors Carlo Mangoni and Luciano d'Ambrosio from the Second University of Naples.

Ciro a Santa Brigida has been in this elegant quarter since 1932, opened by Antonio's grandfather Don Carmine Pace, who moved his grandfather's restaurant from Via Foria. It quickly became the meeting place of the elite who frequented the opera house and the upscale commercial area surrounding it.

At eighty-eight, Antonio's father, Vincenzo Pace, is the oldest living *pizzaiolo*. Before World War I, he worked in his grandfather's *pizzeria* in the center of Naples. He is credited with inventing the idea of *stagione* pizza and separating the quadrants with strips of dough. Antonio Pace explains the uniqueness of Neapolitan pizza: "The most important thing is that the dough is good. Pizza is the dough. With the addition of the other ingredients, it becomes the mother, Margherita, or the father, marinara."

The DOC pizza here is called *oro*, which means gold. As in all of the other *pizzerie*, the price is higher for the DOC. When you order the Margherita, there is no question whether the mozzarella is made from water buffalo's milk or cow's milk. Professor d'Ambrosio tells us a favorite adage: "When we say *mozzarella* we mean bufala; when we say *pizza*, we mean Napoli."

Tradition hasn't stopped here with pizza; we are invited to try the typical local wines that best accompany pizza. Professor Mangoni prefers the local white wine, Asprinio, with marinara, and the bubbly red Gragnano with Margherita. I ask Professor Mangoni why he has such an intense interest in pizza. "I am interested in all things Neapolitan," he says. "My family has been here for nine hundred years. It's not that I disapprove of unusual toppings or variations in the crust, I just believe that those pizzas should not be called Neapolitan."

We finish our pizza *degustazione* with one of the early Neapolitan pizzas, *cecinielli*, with larval white fish sprinkled liberally on top. As I leave, Pasquale Parziale, Maestro Pizzaiolo, presents me with his card. Dressed snappily in a white jacket and tie, he is overseeing the work of an apprentice. If I read his address correctly, he lives on Via Regina Margherita—how appropriate!

Pizza at Home —Cooking in a Wood-Burning Oven

Up until the last decade, short of a trip to Italy, your best opportunity to have a wood-fired pizza was in a restaurant. Now, there are a few companies importing or producing ovens suited to a residential setting (see Resources, page 108). The ideal oven is made of porous refractory clay, high in alumina, a mineral that promotes fast and even heat distribution. Beware of ovens made of concrete or concrete-clay mix, as they tend to crack under high temperatures.

Before you decide that a wood-burning oven is an extravagance, remember that it is used not only for pizza. Because its heat is hotter and drier, a wood-burning oven is also great for roasting. In fact, as the oven cools down from the pizza cooking level, the temperature falls to just the right level for meats and vegetables, which can be cooked quickly, sealing in natural juices and flavors. Closing the flue then maintains a slow, warm oven perfect for baking breads.

The wood used should be hard, such as oak, maple, or mesquite. Fruit woods or wood chips from apple, almond, cherry, grape, and peach can be added to flavor meat, fish, and poultry. Resinous woods such as pine or spruce should not be used; they don't burn hot enough and will leave a residue on the oven floor.

Cooking in a Conventional Oven

All of the recipes in this book were tested in my 1940s O'Kieffe and Merritt gas oven with a pizza stone inside. Most cookware stores have a variety of pizza stones to choose from. Measure the shelf of your oven and buy the largest stone it will accommodate, leaving a margin of 1 inch around the edges for air circulation. Round stones are space-inefficient, allowing you to cook only one pizza at a time. Be certain that the stone is made of porous material, to absorb moisture and give the crust a crisp finish. Unglazed quarry tiles made of hard red clay work very well. Glazed or sealed tiles are not as good, because they are not porous. Your stone should be at least $1/2$ inch thick—a manageable size that won't take too long to heat up and thick enough to not break easily. For more intense radiant heat, place a stone on the floor of the oven or on the bottom shelf as well.

Your pizza stone needs to be seasoned to prevent cracking at high temperatures. Follow the manufacturer's instruction.

When you're ready to make pizza, preheat the oven with the stone inside for at least 30 minutes or up to 1 hour at 500°F. Use an oven thermometer placed in the area where the pizza will be baked to gauge the heat.

A Note about the Recipes

I used either Fleischmann's brand compressed fresh yeast or bought live yeast from my neighborhood baker. If you use dried granulated yeast in the packets, use half the quantity called for in these recipes. If you are not sure if your yeast is active, proof it in the specified amount of luke-warm or warm water (80° to 90°F for compressed yeast, 105° to 115°F for dry) with a pinch of sugar. Wait for 5 minutes, or until it becomes foamy on top, then proceed. If you do not see a foamy reaction, it is not an active yeast.

I let my dough rise in a stainless steel bowl covered with plastic wrap and placed in my old oven with just the pilot light to warm it. The important thing is that the dough is in a warm and draft-free place.

I like to assemble my pizza directly on the paddle so that I don't disturb the arrangement of ingredients with an extra transfer. A light sprinkling of coarsely ground semolina, flour, or cornmeal helps keep the dough from sticking to the paddle. The little grains act like ball bearings to help it slide onto the pizza stone.

~

*Classic
Pizza
Napoletana*

~

Classic Pizza Napoletana

The *Progetto di Norma*, the proposal for DOC compliance for *verace pizza napoletana,* is a bit technical. It is intended to provide a definition for the two types of *verace pizza napoletana*, marinara and Margherita, to specify the raw materials used in those pizzas, and to list the methods of producing them. *Pizzerie* that offer these pizzas on their menus must abide strictly to the standards set forth. In return, they may display the logo signifying that they are in conformity. Here is a brief summary of the high points:

Defining Traditional DOC Pizza

Verace Pizza Napoletana

A food product made with the specific raw materials detailed below, following the outlined process of production, and supported by a risen dough garnished with tomato and oil to compose the two types, marinara and Margherita, and the two variations.

Verace Pizza Napoletana Marinara

Pizza garnished with tomatoes, oil, oregano, and garlic.

Verace Pizza Napoletana Margherita

Pizza garnished with tomatoes, oil, mozzarella, and basil.

Verace Pizza Napoletana Margherita Classica

Pizza garnished with tomatoes, oil, mozzarella, basil, and grated Parmigiano-Reggiano, pecorino, or grana padano.

Verace Pizza Napoletana Margherita Extra

Pizza garnished with tomatoes, fresh cherry tomatoes, mozzarella, oil, and basil.

Approved Ingredients

Flour

The DOC document for *pizza napoletana* goes into a detailed description of the appropriate flour, *farina di grano tenero tipo 00*, literally "flour of soft grain, type 00." *Grano tenero* is used for breads and pastries while high-protein hard wheat, *grano duro*, is used to make semolina flour for dried pasta. In Italy, the types of flour are graded according to the refining process, rather than the American system of rating by protein content. Tipo 00 is the most refined and contains the least fiber; it has a protein content of 11 to 12.5 percent. Tipo 0 has had 70 percent of the fiber removed; Tipo 1 and Tipo 2 have increasing amounts of husk and germ; and *integrale* uses the whole wheat berry and varies only in the consistency of the coarseness of milling.

Tipo 00 is a silky white flour, lower in protein than American all-purpose flour, which is why the pizza dough is so soft and tender. In reality, I saw bags of flour from Manitoba, Canada, in the kitchens of many *pizzerie*, indicating that they use at least a portion of higher-protein flour. The advantage of high-protein flour is the enhanced development of gluten, the reaction of glutenin and glyadin that is activated when moisture is added and the dough is kneaded. Gluten gives the dough an elastic property that is essential in forming a dough structure that will hold its shape as it rises. When using a lower-protein flour, the dough needs to be kneaded longer, which is why the DOC regulations indicate a mixing and kneading time of at least 30 minutes.

In *The Italian Baker*, Carol Field recommends using one part pastry flour to three parts all-purpose flour to approximate Tipo 00 flour. I have used a smaller proportion in the recipes that follow, but you might want to experiment to achieve the crust that suits your taste. (See Resources, page 108, for places to buy Tipo 00 flour.)

Salt

Even though all but one of Italy's regions meet the sea, salt has always been a precious commodity. A government monopoly, salt was an expensive, controlled substance, subject to government tax, and sold only in the tobacco stores. In poor times, cooks often resorted to using seawater for cooking or found ingredients such as anchovies or capers preserved in salt, or salt-cured meats such as prosciutto, to replace the salt in their cooking.

Although sea salt is the DOC specified salt for *pizza napoletana*, regular table salt can be substituted. Salt is used in a large quantity to boost the elasticity of the gluten and to slow the action of the yeast.

Yeast

Yeast is a living entity. The pizzaioli in Naples use *lievito di birra fresco*, or fresh beer yeast. The brewers' yeast we see here is something different. The most comparable thing here is compressed fresh yeast, which usually comes in foil-wrapped 1/2-ounce cubes. Cake yeast has a relatively short shelf life, so check expiration dates when buying. Your neighborhood baker may be able to sell you some fresh cake yeast.

Water

There is something about the water in Naples. It would probably be impractical to use imported bottled water for pizza making, but for the purist, it may be something to consider. The water is hard, full of minerals, and makes the best espresso I've ever had. According to the Pizza Napoletana DOC, the pH of the water in Naples is 6.7. At home, I use filtered water for drinking and cooking to avoid chlorine and impurities in the tap water.

Tomatoes

The first documentation of tomatoes in Italy was a description by Pietro Andrea Mattioli in 1544. He called them *pomi d'oro*, golden apples. At that time they were used only as an ornamental plant, and most people thought they were either toxic, or at best, an aphrodisiac. It wasn't until the seventeenth century that tomatoes found their way into the kitchen. Professor Carlo Mangoni speculates that the tomato came together with bread sometime around 1760. In 1778, Vincenzo Corrado published the book *Il Cuoco Galante*, which included several recipes with tomatoes. The first published recipe for pasta with tomato sauce, *vermicelli con le pomodoro*, appeared in Naples in 1839.

In 1875, the industrial production of tomatoes was led by Francesco Cirio, who created Salsa Cirio, one of the first canned tomato goods.

In the Nocerino-Sarnese area of Campania, where the provinces of Naples, Salerno, and Avellino meet, lie the San Marzano fields. The volcanic soil, rich in minerals, aided by the sunny southern climate, yields four crop rotations a year. The tomato variety San Marzano (*Lycopersicon esculentum*) is a cylindrical, two-lobed fruit. It is probably a hybrid derived from two earlier varieties, *fiaschella* and *fiascone,* that originated in the early 1800s. They are tall, highly productive plants bearing up to a dozen bunches of five to six tomatoes in a 60-day growing period. This is the

The preferred tomato for pizza napoletana is the San Marzano variety (Lycopersicon esculentum). Grown in volcanic soil, it is a hybrid that originated in the early 1800s. In season, pizzerie use fresh tomatoes, but in the winter, canned tomatoes are substituted.

preferred tomato for *pizza napoletana* due to its low-acid, full-tomato flavor. The San Marzano, similar to what we call plum (Roma) tomatoes, is meatier and drier with few seeds and a bright red skin that is easily removed.

The DOC regulations for *pizza napoletana* have specific guidelines for tomatoes. The first important stipulation is that the tomatoes can be either fresh or canned. When fresh tomatoes are not in season, canned peeled tomatoes are a perfectly acceptable substitute.

Fresh tomatoes must be one of the three following varieties: San Marzano, or a similar elongated type from the region, or Corbara or Carbarini, both small (about 1 inch in diameter), bright red, round tomatoes with an apex that comes to a sharp point. They are often seen hanging in clusters in *pizzerie.*

Canned tomatoes must be of superior quality, preferably San Marzano. The drained product must be at least 70 percent of the net weight. It is acceptable to use products with partially concentrated tomato juice as long as it does not exceed the quantity of drained tomatoes.

Oil

According to Professor Mangoni, in the past either olive oil or rendered pork fat was used. Now, however, the DOC specifies the use of extra-virgin olive oil from southern Italy. This local olive oil is rich and full-bodied, sweet, and never bitter.

Garlic and Herbs

The only two herbs used for *pizza napoletana* are fresh basil and dried oregano. Fresh garlic is used only on the pizza marinara.

Cheese

Mozzarella falls into the category of cheeses called *pasta filata,* which are made by the process of cooking the curds in boiling water, tearing the mass into strips, and then shaping it by stretching or kneading. It is a magnificent fresh cheese, highly perishable and best consumed within 48 hours.

In Naples, when someone says *mozzarella* they are only speaking of the mozzarella made from the milk of the water buffalo; cow's milk mozzarella is called *fior di latte.*

Mozzarella di bufala is higher in fat and protein and contains more liquid. Professor Mangoni recommends, "When using *mozzarella di bufala* on pizza, it is best to use day-old cheese that has lost some of its moisture, and be sure to avoid the machine-made mozzarella for pizza."

The DOC Margherita classica allows the use of grated Parmigiano-Reggiano, grana padano, or pecorino.

Parmigiano-Reggiano is a cow's milk cheese that has aged at least 18 months. Grana padano, also made from cow's milk, is aged a minimum of 12 months. Pecorino is made from sheep's milk and aged for 12 months.

Production

The dough must contain only flour, water, salt, and natural yeast (no oil or fat). It must be mixed and kneaded by hand or with approved mixers, ones that won't heat the dough up, for at least 30 minutes. The first rising in bulk is at least 4 hours. Balls of 180 grams are formed and left to rise for 2 to 4 hours. The temperature for rising should be approximately 75°F. The dough will be fat and smooth. Each ball is stretched until the center is $1/2$ centimeter (about $1/4$ inch) thick. The outer rim (*cornicione*) is left

slightly thicker to hold the ingredients inside.

The pizza should not exceed 30 centimeters (about 12 inches) in diameter. It must be baked on the floor of an oven made of refractory brick or stone and fueled by nonaromatic hardwood to a temperature of 750°–800°F. When finished, it must not be crusty, but should be well done, with a soft high edge. On the following pages are recipes for the classic Neapolitan DOC pizzas.

~ *Classic Pizza Dough DOC* ~

This is the classic dough for making Neapolitan-style pizza. If you are short on time, try the Quick-Rise Pizza Dough on page 48. It uses yeast in larger quantites and requires less time to rise.

1/2 cake compressed fresh yeast

2 cups warm water (80°–90°F)

1 cup pastry flour

1-1/2 tablespoons sea salt

5-1/2 to 6 cups unbleached all-purpose flour

In the bowl of a heavy-duty mixer fitted with a dough hook, stir the yeast into the warm water until it dissolves. Add the 1 cup pastry flour and the salt and mix well. Add the all-purpose flour 1 cup at a time, kneading until the dough is not sticky, about 10 minutes. Continue to knead for about 20 minutes longer, or until the dough is smooth and elastic.

For the first rising, shape the dough into a ball and leave it in the mixer or place it on a lightly floured work surface. Cover with a towel and let rise in a warm, draft-free place (75°F) for 4 hours.

Punch the dough down and divide it into 6 pieces. Form each piece into a ball. Cover with a towel and let rise in a warm (75°F), draft-free place for 2 to 4 hours, until doubled. *Makes enough dough for six 10-inch pizzas*

~ *Pizza Marinara DOC* ~

San Marzano is the preferred tomato for making DOC pizzas.
Plum tomatoes such as Roma, or a similar elongated type from Campania, can also be used.
Out of season, use superior-quality canned tomatoes, preferably San Marzano.

Classic Pizza Dough DOC (page 39)
8 ounces fresh tomatoes, coarsely chopped, or 8 ounces
canned tomatoes, drained and chopped
6 cloves garlic, sliced thin

3/4 teaspoon dried oregano
Sea salt to taste
3 tablespoons extra-virgin olive oil

Preheat a wood-burning pizza oven to 750°F.

Pat and then stretch each ball of dough to a thickness of 1/4 inch, leaving the outer edge, the *cornicione*, slightly thicker. Each round will be about 10 inches in diameter. Place the rounds on a flour-dusted pizza paddle. Place some of the tomatoes in the center of each dough round and with a circular motion, spread it uniformly over the round, leaving a 1/2-inch rim. Sprinkle the garlic on top of the tomatoes. Distribute the oregano and sea salt evenly over the top of the pizzas. Drizzle olive oil in a spiral motion from the center to the outer edge.

Slide each assembled pizza onto the floor of the oven and bake for 1 to 1-1/2 minutes, or until the edges are golden brown. Remove from the oven and serve at once.

Makes six 10-inch pizzas; serves 6

~

The first classic Pizza Margherita was made, or at least named, by Raffaele Esposito of Pietro il Pizzaiolo pizzeria, now called Pizzeria Brandi. In 1889, Esposito was invited to the palace to create three pizzas for the visit of King Umberto and Queen Margherita of Savoy. The queen declared that her favorite was the patriotic one resembling the Italian flag with its colors of red (tomatoes), white (mozzarella cheese), and green (basil).

~

~ *Pizza Margherita DOC* ~

The DOC regulations allow only two variations on the definition of Pizza Margherita.
One, called Pizza Margherita Classica DOC, includes the optional use of 1/4 cup grated Parmigiano-Reggiano,
pecorino romano, or grana padano cheese. Sprinkle it over the tomatoes and mozzarella before baking.

Classic Pizza Dough (page 39)
7 ounces fresh tomatoes, coarsely chopped, or 7 ounces
canned tomatoes, drained and chopped

12 ounces mozzarella di bufala, cut into 1/4-inch-thick slices
Sea salt to taste
25 to 30 fresh basil leaves
2 tablespoons extra-virgin olive oil

Preheat a wood-burning pizza oven to 750°F.

Pat and then stretch each ball of dough to a thickness of 1/4 inch, leaving the outer edge, the *cornicione*, slightly thicker. Each round will be about 10 inches in diameter. Place the rounds on a flour-dusted pizza paddle. Place some of the tomatoes in the center of each dough round and with a circular motion, spread it uniformly over the round, leaving a 1/2-inch rim. Distribute the mozzarella evenly over the surface of the tomatoes. Sprinkle each pizza evenly with sea salt and top with 2 or 3 leaves of basil. Drizzle olive oil in a spiral motion from the center to the outer edge.

Slide each assembled pizza onto the pizza stone and bake for 1 to 1-1/2 minutes, or until the edges are golden brown. Remove from the oven, top each pizza with the remaining basil leaves, and serve at once. *Makes six 10-inch pizzas; serves 6*

~ *Pizza Margherita Extra DOC* ~

Margherita Extra is one of the variations allowed for Pizza Margherita.
It uses a smaller amount of tomato sauce and adds fresh sliced tomatoes. The fresh tomatoes are usually
the Corbara or Carbarini, both small (about 1 inch in diameter), red cherry tomatoes.

Classic Pizza Dough (page 39)
4 ounces fresh tomatoes, coarsely chopped, or 4 ounces
canned tomatoes, drained and chopped
12 ounces fresh cherry tomatoes, cut into
1/4-inch-thick slices

16 ounces mozzarella di bufala, cut into
1/4-inch-thick slices
30 fresh basil leaves
Sea salt to taste
2 tablespoons extra-virgin olive oil

Preheat a wood-burning pizza oven to 750°F.

Pat and then stretch each ball of dough to a thickness of 1/4 inch, leaving the outer edge, the *cornicione,* slightly thicker. Each round will be about 10 inches in diameter. Place the rounds on a flour-dusted pizza paddle. Place some of the chopped tomatoes in the center of the dough disk and, with a circular motion, spread it uniformly over the round, leaving 1/2-inch rim.

Distribute the mozzarella evenly over the surface of the tomatoes. Make a layer of sliced cherry tomatoes on top of the mozzarella. Sprinkle each pizza evenly with sea salt and top with 2 or 3 leaves of basil. Drizzle olive oil in a spiral motion from the center to the outer edge.

Slide each pizza onto the pizza stone and bake for 1 to 1-1/2 minutes, or until the edges are golden brown. Remove from the oven, garnish with the remaining basil leaves, and serve at once. *Makes six 10-inch pizzas; serves 6*

~

Nothing in the DOC regulations says that the pizza must be made in Naples, much less Italy. Any restaurant in the world can make the guarantee that their production of the two pizzas meets the requirements of the DOC. In the United States, Peppe Miele's Antica Pizzeria is the only U.S. member of Associazione Vera Pizza Napoletana. His pizzeria has been producing wood-burning Neapolitan pizza since 1992 (8022 West Third Street, Los Angeles, California).

~

~

Neapolitan
Pizzeria
Specialties

~

~ *Quick-Rise Pizza Dough* ~

This dough only takes about two hours to make, and is reminiscent of the DOC dough.
For a softer, more Neapolitan-like dough, substitute 1 cup of the all-purpose flour with pastry flour.

1 cake compressed fresh yeast, or 1 package active dry yeast

2 cups lukewarm or warm water (80° to 90°F for compressed yeast, 105° to 115°F for dry yeast)

1 cup pastry flour

4 teaspoons sea salt

5-1/2 to 6 cups unbleached all-purpose flour

In the bowl of a heavy-duty mixer fitted with a dough hook, stir the yeast in the lukewarm or warm water until dissolved. Add the pastry flour and salt and mix well. Continue kneading, adding the all-purpose flour 1 cup at a time, until the dough is smooth and not sticky, about 10 minutes.

Shape the dough into a ball and put in a lightly oiled bowl. Turn the ball to coat it with oil. Cover with plastic wrap and let rise in a warm (75°F), draft-free place for 1 hour, or until doubled in volume.

Punch the dough down and divide it into 6 balls weighing about 6 ounces each. Place the balls on parchment paper or a lightly floured work surface, cover with a towel, and let rise for 45 minutes, or until doubled in volume. *Makes enough dough for six 10-inch pizzas*

Note: *Flavored Pizza Dough*
One or more of the following additions can be kneaded into any pizza dough before the second rise: 1 tablespoon fresh minced herbs, such as rosemary, dill, or thyme; 2 oil-packed sun-dried tomatoes, drained and minced; 1/4 cup minced scallions; 2 cloves garlic, minced; 1 ounce prosciutto di Parma, minced; 2 teaspoons grated lemon zest.

~ *Pizza-Maker's Sauce* ~

While a simple tomato puree is the most common sauce for pizza napoletana, *many Neapolitan* pizzerie
*also use flavored sauces such as this one. This wonderful herb and vegetable flavored sauce is especially adapted for pizzas
cooked in conventional ovens. Any extra sauce can be frozen, used on pasta, or as a dip for toasted bread.*

3 tablespoons extra-virgin olive oil

1/2 cup diced onion

1 carrot, peeled and diced

1 stalk celery, diced

2 cloves garlic, minced

*One 28-ounce can Italian tomatoes,
coarsely chopped*

4 fresh basil leaves, minced

1 tablespoon minced fresh flat-leaf parsley

Sea salt and freshly ground pepper to taste

In a skillet over medium-high heat, heat the olive oil. Sauté the onion, carrot, and celery until golden brown, 4 to 5 minutes. Add the garlic and cook until softened, about 2 minutes. Stir in the tomatoes and their juice, the basil, and parsley. Reduce heat to a simmer and cook until thickened, 15 to 20 minutes. Place in a blender or food processor and blend until smooth. Season with salt and pepper and set aside to cool until ready to use. *Makes 4 cups*

~ *Pizza Capasso* ~

ARTICHOKE AND SWEET PEPPER PIZZA

Red and yellow peppers are a colorful addition to this summer pizza. Artichoke hearts marinated
in oil can be substituted for fresh.

6 baby artichokes

1/2 lemon

Classic Pizza Dough (page 39) or Quick-Rise
Pizza Dough (page 48)

Extra-virgin olive oil for brushing

6 ounces fior di latte (cow's milk) mozzarella,
sliced very thin

1 red bell pepper, roasted, peeled, and julienned

1 yellow bell pepper, roasted, peeled, and julienned

1/2 cup coarsely grated Parmigiano-Reggiano cheese

Bring 2 inches of water in a large pot to a boil. Trim the tops of the artichokes. Remove the coarse outer leaves and trim the stem. Rub all cut surfaces with the lemon. Place the artichokes in the water. Squeeze the lemon half over the artichokes and drop the lemon into the water. Reduce heat to low, cover, and cook for 10 to 12 minutes, or until the artichokes are tender and a leaf can be easily pulled off. Drain and let cool. Remove the outer leaves and the choke. Cut the artichoke hearts into quarters and set aside.

Preheat an oven to 500°F for at least 30 minutes with a pizza stone inside.

Pat, and then stretch each ball of dough to a thickness

of 1/4 inch, leaving the outer edge, the *cornicione*, slightly thicker. Each round will be about 10 inches in diameter. Place each round on flour-dusted pizza paddle. Lightly brush the surface of the dough with the olive oil. Divide the mozzarella evenly among the rounds, spreading to cover the surface but leaving a 1/2-inch rim. Distribute the artichoke hearts and roasted peppers evenly among the pizzas. Sprinkle the Parmigiano-Reggiano evenly over the top of the artichokes and peppers.

Slide the pizzas onto the pizza stone and bake for 4 to 5 minutes, or until the edges are golden brown. Remove from the oven and serve at once. *Makes six 10-inch pizzas; serves 6*

~ *Quattro Stagione alla Pizzeria Gorizia* ~

FOUR SEASONS PIZZA

In this version of the classic, spring is asparagus, summer is zucchini, fall is olives, and

winter is potatoes. Come up with your own seasonal variation, or just choose any four different toppings.

The quadrants can be divided by a strip of dough rolled into a thin rope.

*Classic Pizza Dough (page 39) or Quick-Rise
Pizza Dough (page 48)
1 cup Pizza-Maker's Sauce (page 49)
6 ounces fior di latte (cow's milk) mozzarella,
sliced very thin*

*1/2 cup shredded Parmigiano-Reggiano cheese
8 ounces asparagus tips, blanched
1 potato, peeled, sliced 1/4 inch thick, and blanched
1 cup Italian or Greek black olives
1 zucchini, sliced 1/4 inch thick, and blanched*

Preheat an oven to 500°F for at least 30 minutes with a pizza stone inside.

Pat, and then stretch each ball of dough to a thickness of 1/4 inch, leaving the outer edge, the *cornicione*, slightly thicker. Each round will be about 10 inches in diameter. Place each round on flour-dusted pizza paddle. Place some of the sauce in the center of each pizza, spreading to cover the surface, but leaving a 1/2-inch rim. Divide the mozzarella evenly among the rounds. Distribute the Parmigiano-Reggiano evenly over the top of the mozzarella. Arrange the asparagus, potato, olives, and zucchini over the cheeses in 4 quadrants.

Slide the pizzas onto the pizza stone and bake for 4 to 5 minutes, or until the edges are golden brown. Remove from the oven and serve at once. *Makes six 10-inch pizzas; serves 6*

~ *Pizza Cantanapoli* ~

"EIGHT SEASONS" PIZZA

This is a variation of the four seasons pizza with twice as many tastes. It is the house pizza of Pizzeria Cantanapoli.

8 ounces ground pork

1 egg

1 tablespoon minced fresh flat-leaf parsley

1 slice stale bread, soaked in 1/2 cup milk

Salt and freshly ground pepper to taste

8 ounces eggplant

3 tablespoons extra-virgin olive oil, plus more for drizzling

Classic Pizza Dough (page 39) or Quick-Rise Pizza

Dough (page 48), shaped into 4 balls before the second rise

1 cup Pizza-Maker's Sauce (page 49)

6 ounces fior di latte (cow's milk) mozzarella,

sliced very thin

8 ounces mushrooms, stemmed and thinly sliced

10 cherry tomatoes, cut in half

1-1/2 cup cauliflower florets, blanched

8 ounces medium shrimp, peeled and deveined

1/2 cup coarsely grated Parmigiano-Reggiano cheese

6 hard-boiled eggs, peeled and cut in half lengthwise

Preheat an oven to 500°F for at least 30 minutes with a pizza stone inside.

In a bowl, combine the pork, egg, parsley, bread, salt, and pepper. Shape into 1/2-inch balls and set aside.

Cut the eggplant into 1/2-inch dice. Generously salt on both sides and let drain on paper towels for at least 15 minutes. Rinse and pat dry. In a skillet over medium-high heat, heat the olive oil. Add the eggplant and sauté 3 to 4 minutes. Season with salt and pepper to taste and set aside.

Pat, then stretch 3 of the balls of dough into 15-inch rounds, 1/4 inch thick. Divide the remaining ball into 12 pieces and roll each piece into a strip 15 inches long. Place each round on a flour-dusted pizza paddle. Spread some of the sauce in the center of each pizza, leaving a 1/2-inch outer rim. Form 8 quadrants by placing 4 strips of dough on each pizza. Place a different ingredient in each quadrant, leaving one quadrant empty to add the hard-boiled eggs after baking. Sprinkle the Parmigiano-Reggiano evenly over the top, and drizzle with olive oil.

Bake the pizzas on the pizza stone for 4 to 5 minutes. Remove from the oven, add the hard-boiled eggs, and serve at once. *Makes three 15-inch pizzas, serves 6*

~ Pizza Caprese de Don Salvatore ~

PIZZA WITH MOZZARELLA AND GREEN TOMATOES

Italians enjoy green tomatoes in their salads, so it is no surprise to find them in other dishes as well.
The tartness of the tomato accents the smooth mozzarella well.

Classic Pizza Dough (page 39) or Quick-Rise
Pizza Dough (page 48)
2 tablespoons extra-virgin olive oil for
brushing, plus oil for drizzling

10 ounces mozzarella di bufala, sliced 1/4 inch thick
5 green tomatoes, sliced 1/4 inch thick
1/2 cup coarsely grated Parmigiano-Reggiano cheese
Sea salt to taste

Preheat an oven to 500°F for at least 30 minutes with a pizza stone inside.

Pat, and then stretch each ball of dough to a thickness of 1/4 inch, leaving the outer edge, the *cornicione*, slightly thicker. Each round will be about 10 inches in diameter. Place each round on a flour-dusted pizza paddle. Lightly brush each pizza with olive oil. Divide the mozzarella evenly among the rounds. Distribute the sliced tomatoes evenly over the top and sprinkle with the Parmigiano-Reggiano. Season with salt and drizzle olive oil over the top.

Slide the pizzas onto the pizza stone and bake for 4 to 5 minutes, or until the edges are golden brown. Remove from the oven and serve at once. *Makes six 10-inch pizzas; serves 6*

~ *Pizza con Uovo* ~

PIZZA WITH AN EGG

Pizza is available any time of the day in Naples, with just about any topping you prefer.
This pizza sounds like breakfast, but it would also make a good appetizer.

Classic Pizza Dough (page 39) or Quick-Rise
Pizza Dough (page 48)
3 tablespoons extra-virgin olive oil, plus oil for drizzling

6 eggs
Sea salt and freshly ground pepper to taste
6 tablespoons coarsely grated Parmigiano-Reggiano cheese

Preheat an oven to 500°F for at least 30 minutes with a pizza stone inside.

Pat, then stretch the balls of dough to a thickness of 1/4 inch, rolling the edge to form an extra thick rim. Each round will be about 8 inches in diameter. Place each round on a flour-dusted pizza paddle. Brush the center of the round with olive oil. Crack an egg in the center, season with salt and pepper, and sprinkle with Parmigiano-Reggiano. Drizzle with olive oil.

Carefully slide the pizzas onto the pizza stone and bake for 8 to 9 minutes, or until the egg is set and the edges of the pizzas are golden brown. Remove from the oven and serve at once. *Makes six 8-inch pizzas; serves 6*

~ Ruota di Carretto Forte alla Trianon ~

SPICY GIANT CARTWHEEL

This is a party pizza—make it spicy. If your oven is not large enough to handle
a 30-inch pizza, then make four standard-size pizzas.

2 packages active dry yeast

4 cups warm water (105° to 115°F)

11 to 12 cups unbleached all-purpose flour

3 tablespoons sea salt

2 cups Pizza-Maker's Sauce (page 49)

4 ripe tomatoes, sliced 1/4 inch thick

1 pound spicy sausage, sliced 1/8 inch thick

1/2 cup coarsely chopped, drained oil-marinated roasted peppers

6 cloves garlic, sliced

1 teaspoon crushed red pepper flakes

1/4 cup shredded fresh basil

2 tablespoons minced fresh flat-leaf parsley

In the bowl of a heavy-duty mixer fitted with a dough hook, stir the yeast in the warm water to dissolve. Add 1 cup of the flour and the salt and mix well. Continue kneading and adding the flour 1 cup at a time until the dough is smooth and not sticky, about 10 minutes. Shape the dough into a ball and put in a lightly oiled bowl. Turn the dough to coat it with oil. Cover with plastic wrap and let rise in a warm place (75°F) for 1 hour, or until doubled in volume.

Punch the dough down and divide it into 2 balls. Place the balls on a floured surface, cover with a towel, and let rise for 45 minutes, or until doubled.

Preheat an oven to 500°F for at least 30 minutes to 1 hour with a pizza stone inside.

Pat, then stretch the balls of dough to a thickness of 1/4 inch, leaving the outer edge, the *cornicione*, slightly thicker. Each round will be about 30 inches. Place each round on a flour-dusted pizza paddle. Place 1 cup of the sauce in the center of each pizza, spreading to cover the surface but leaving a 1/2-inch rim. Distribute the tomatoes, sausage, peppers, garlic, and pepper flakes randomly but evenly over the top of the sauce.

Slide the pizzas onto the pizza stone and bake for 4 to 5 minutes, or until the edges are golden brown. Remove from the oven, sprinkle with the basil and parsley, and serve at once. *Makes two 30-inch pizzas; serves 12*

~ Pizza Lasagna alla Trianon ~

TRIANON'S PIZZA LASAGNA

Ciro Leone of Pizzeria Trianon wrote down this recipe for me as follows: Pizza Lasagna: mozzarella, ricotta, prosciutto cotto, pomodoro, and formaggio Romano Pecorino, *all ingredients found in the local hearty lasagna. I came up with some amounts that approximated what I tasted in his pizzeria.*

*Classic Pizza Dough (page 39) or Quick-Rise
Pizza Dough (page 48)
1 cup Pizza-Maker's Sauce (page 49)
1/2 cup ricotta cheese
6 ounces mozzarella di bufala, sliced very thin
3 ounces cooked ham, diced (1/3 cup)*

*3 large Roma (plum) tomatoes, peeled and coarsely chopped
6 tablespoons grated pecorino Romano cheese
1 tablespoon dried oregano
Sea salt to taste
Extra-virgin olive oil for drizzling*

Preheat an oven to 500°F for at least 30 minutes with a pizza stone inside.

Pat, and then stretch each ball of dough to a thickness of 1/4 inch, leaving the outer edge, the *cornicione*, slightly thicker. Each round will be about 10 inches in diameter. Place each round on a flour-dusted pizza paddle. Place some of the sauce in the center of each pizza, spreading to cover the surface but leaving a 1/2-inch rim. Spread the ricotta evenly over the tomato sauce. Distribute the mozzarella, ham, and tomatoes evenly among the rounds. Sprinkle the pecorino Romano and oregano evenly over the top. Season with salt and drizzle with olive oil.

Slide the pizzas onto the pizza stone and bake for 4 to 5 minutes, or until the edges are golden brown. Remove from the oven and serve at once. *Makes six 10-inch pizzas; serves 6*

~ *Pizza alla Lombardi* ~

PROSCIUTTO AND ARUGULA PIZZA

This is the trendy pizza of the moment, and with good reason. The peppery flavor of the local wild arugula is incredible
with the sweet buttery flavor of prosciutto di Parma. Both ingredients go on after the pizza is cooked.

Classic Pizza Dough (page 39) or Quick-Rise
Pizza Dough (page 48)
Extra-virgin olive oil for brushing
8 ounces smoked mozzarella, sliced very thin

1/2 cup coarsely grated Parmigiano-Reggiano cheese
12 thin slices prosciutto di Parma
1 bunch arugula, stemmed, and cut into julienne

Preheat an oven to 500°F for at least 30 minutes with a pizza stone inside.

Pat, and then stretch each ball of dough to a thickness of 1/4 inch, leaving the outer edge, the *cornicione*, slightly thicker. Each round will be about 10 inches in diameter. Place each round on a flour-dusted pizza paddle. Lightly brush the dough with the olive oil. Divide the smoked mozzarella evenly among the rounds, spreading to cover the surface but leaving a 1/2-inch rim. Distribute the Parmigiano-Reggiano evenly over the top of the mozzarella.

Slide the pizzas onto the pizza stone and bake for 4 to 5 minutes, or until the edges are golden brown. Remove from the oven and top each pizza with 2 slices of prosciutto and a generous pinch of arugula. Serve at once. *Makes six 10-inch pizzas; serves 6*

In the fall,
the forests and hillsides
of Italy are foraged
daily by porcini lovers.
These earthy
mushrooms show up
in every course of
the meal, from salads
with sliced raw porcini
drizzled with fresh
olive oil and lemon juice,
to rich soups and pasta
sauces. Often, grilled
porcini, basted with
garlic and fresh herbs,
will serve as a hearty
main course.

~ Pizza Boscaiola all'Lombardi ~

MUSHROOM PIZZA

In the fall, the forests of Italy are dotted with mushroom hunters. Porcini is on everyone's mind.

Other wild mushrooms, such as shiitakes and morels, may be substituted.

3 tablespoons extra-virgin olive oil

1/2 cup coarsely chopped onion

1 pound porcini or other fresh mushrooms, stemmed and sliced 1/4 inch thick

1/2 cup heavy cream

1 tablespoon minced fresh flat-leaf parsley

2 teaspoons minced fresh thyme

Salt and freshly ground pepper to taste

Classic Pizza Dough (page 39) or Quick-Rise Pizza Dough (page 48)

12 ounces smoked mozzarella, sliced very thin

5 tablespoons coarsely grated Parmigiano-Reggiano cheese

Preheat an oven to 500°F for at least 30 minutes with a pizza stone inside.

In a skillet over medium-high heat, heat the olive oil. Sauté the onion until softened but not browned, 3 to 4 minutes. Add the mushrooms and cook until tender, 4 to 5 minutes. Stir in the cream, parsley, and thyme. Continue to cook until the cream is slightly thickened, 3 to 4 minutes. Season with salt and pepper and remove from heat to cool.

Pat, and then stretch each ball of dough to a thickness of 1/4 inch, leaving the outer edge, the *cornicione*, slightly thicker. Each round will be about 10 inches in diameter. Place each round on a flour-dusted pizza paddle. Divide the smoked mozzarella evenly among the 6 rounds, spreading to cover the surface but leaving a 1/2-inch rim. Distribute the mushroom mixture evenly over the top of the mozzarella. Sprinkle with the Parmigiano-Reggiano.

Slide the pizzas onto the pizza stone and bake for 4 to 5 minutes, or until the edges are golden brown. Remove from the oven and serve at once. *Makes six 10-inch pizzas; serves 6*

~ *Pizza con Salsiccia e Friarielli di Pizzeria Trianon* ~

SAUSAGE AND FRIARIELLI PIZZA

Friarielli, a bitter green in the cabbage family, is not generally available outside Italy, but broccoli rabe is a good substitute. Swiss chard or spinach is also quite tasty.

3 tablespoons extra-virgin olive oil, plus
oil for brushing
1/2 cup chopped onion
3 cloves garlic, sliced
8 ounces sweet ground pork sausage
1/2 cup dry white wine

6 ounces broccoli rabe, coarsely chopped
2 tablespoons minced fresh flat-leaf parsley
Sea salt and freshly ground pepper to taste
Pinch of crushed red pepper flakes
Classic Pizza Dough (page 39) or Quick-Rise
Pizza Dough (page 48)

In a skillet over medium-high heat, heat the 3 tablespoons olive oil. Add the onion and garlic and sauté until softened but not browned. Add the sausage and continue to cook, stirring occasionally, until the meat has lightly browned.

Add the wine, broccoli rabe, and parsley and continue to cook until the wine has reduced and the rabe is tender, 4 to 5 minutes. Season with salt, pepper, and pepper flakes. Set aside.

Preheat an oven to 500°F for at least 30 minutes with a pizza stone inside.

Pat, and then stretch each ball of dough to a thickness of 1/4 inch, leaving the outer edge, the *cornicione*, slightly thicker. Each round will be about 10 inches in diameter. Place each round on a flour-dusted pizza paddle. Brush each pizza with olive oil, leaving a 1/2-inch rim. Distribute the sausage mixture evenly among the pizzas.

Slide the pizzas onto the pizza stone and bake for 4 to 5 minutes, or until the edges are golden brown. Remove from the oven and serve at once. *Makes six 10-inch pizzas; serves 6*

~ Pizza Oro con Funghi e Prosciutto Cotto, Ciro a Santa Brigida ~

MARGHERITA PIZZA WITH MUSHROOMS AND HAM

Antonio Pace, president of the Associazione Vera Pizza Napoletana, calls his DOC pizza oro, *which means gold, referring to the high standard of quality. He also offers a variety of optional ingredients that can be added to the DOC pizzas: arugula, mushrooms, ham, fresh tomato, or anchovies.*

Classic Pizza Dough (page 39)
8 ounces pureed fresh Roma (plum) tomatoes or canned
Italian tomatoes
12 ounces mozzarella di bufala, cut into 1/4-inch-thick slices
8 ounces mushrooms, stemmed and sliced

12 ounces cooked ham, diced (1-1/3 cup)
1/4 cup grated Parmigiano-Reggiano cheese
Sea salt to taste
30 fresh basil leaves
Extra-virgin olive oil for drizzling

Preheat an oven to 500°F for at least 30 minutes with a pizza stone inside.

Pat, and then stretch each ball of dough to a thickness of 1/4 inch, leaving the outer edge, the *cornicione*, slightly thicker. Each round will be about 10 inches in diameter. Place each round on a flour-dusted pizza paddle.

Place some of the tomato puree in the center of the dough rounds, and with a circular motion, spread it uniformly over each round, leaving 1/2 inch rim.

Distribute the mozzarella, mushrooms, and ham evenly over the surface of the puree. Sprinkle each round with Parmigiano-Reggiano cheese, sea salt, and 2 or 3 basil leaves.

Drizzle olive oil in a spiral motion from the center to the outer edge of each round. Slide the assembled pizzas onto the pizza stone and bake for 1 to 1-1/2 minutes, or until the edges are golden brown. Remove from the oven, top with the remaining basil leaves, and serve at once. *Makes six 10-inch pizzas; serves 6*

~ Pizza all'Ortolana Port'Alba ~

GARDEN PIZZA

It is easy to work up an appetite exploring the bookshops between Piazza Dante and Port'Alba. This pizzeria was the first to open in Naples, and it is still a meeting place for the intellectuals, artists, and students of the quarter.

*Classic Pizza Dough (page 39) or Quick-Rise
Pizza Dough (page 48)
1 cup Pizza-Maker's Sauce (page 49)
8 ounces fior di latte (cow's milk) mozzarella, sliced very thin
1/2 cup coarsely grated Parmigiano-Reggiano cheese*

*1 cup thinly sliced broccoli rabe, blanched
3 Roma (plum) tomatoes, sliced 1/4 inch thick
8 ounces portobello mushrooms, stemmed and
sliced 1/4 inch thick
1 onion, sliced 1/4 inch thick*

Preheat an oven to 500°F for at least 30 minutes with a pizza stone inside.

Pat, and then stretch each ball of dough to a thickness of 1/4 inch, leaving the outer edge, the *cornicione*, slightly thicker. Each round will be about 10 inches in diameter. Place each round on a flour-dusted pizza paddle. Place some of the sauce in the center of each pizza, spreading to cover the surface but leaving a 1/2-inch rim. Divide the mozzarella evenly among the rounds. Distribute the Parmigiano-Reggiano evenly over the top of the mozzarella. Arrange the broccoli rabe, tomatoes, mushrooms, and onion in concentric circles over the cheeses.

Slide the pizzas onto the pizza stone and bake for 4 to 5 minutes, or until the edges are golden brown. Remove from the oven and serve at once. *Makes six 10-inch pizzas; serves 6*

~ *Pizza Pescatore della Pizzeria Brandi* ~

SEAFOOD PIZZA

This is a cheeseless pizza, as Italians seldom use cheese with seafood. It should have the freshest local seafood you can get.

*3 tablespoons extra-virgin olive oil, plus
more for drizzling
1/2 cup chopped onion
3 cloves garlic, minced
1 cup dry white wine
1/4 cup minced fresh flat-leaf parsley
1 pound fresh mussels, scrubbed and debearded*

*Classic Pizza Dough (page 39) or Quick-Rise
Pizza Dough (page 48)
1 cup Pizza-Maker's Sauce (page 49)
8 ounces medium shrimp, peeled and deveined
8 ounces squid, cleaned and cut into 1/4-inch-thick rings
8 ounces fresh sea bass, cut into 1-inch chunks
1/4 cup salt-cured capers, rinsed and drained*

In a large, heavy skillet over medium-high heat, heat the olive oil. Add the onion and garlic and sauté until softened but not browned. Add the wine, parsley, and mussels. Cover and cook over high heat, until all of the mussels have opened, about 5 minutes. With a slotted spoon, remove the mussels and set aside to cool. Discard any mussels that have not opened. Strain and reserve the cooked onion mixture.

Remove the mussels from the shells, reserving all the deeper shell halves. Trim away the valves and return the mussels to the half shells. Spoon 1 teaspoon of the reserved onion mixture on top and set aside.

Preheat an oven to 500°F for at least 30 minutes with a pizza stone inside.

Pat, and then stretch each ball of dough to a thickness of 1/4 inch, leaving the outer edge, the *cornicione*, slightly thicker. Each round will be about 10 inches in diameter. Place each round on a flour-dusted pizza paddle. Place some of the sauce in the center of each pizza, spreading to cover the surface but leaving a 1/2-inch rim. Arrange the shrimp, squid, and sea bass in quadrants, leaving one quadrant empty for the later addition of the cooked mussels. Drizzle the seafood with olive oil. Slide the pizzas onto the pizza stone and bake for 4 to 5 minutes, or until the edges are golden brown. Remove from the oven, place the mussels in their shells on the empty quadrant and sprinkle the capers on top. Serve at once. *Makes six 10-inch pizzas; serves 6*

Capers are the
unopened bud of a
scrubby Mediterranean
bush. They grow wild
out of rock walls and
castle ramparts all over
central and southern
Italy, but the best ones
come from the volcanic
islands surrounding
Sicily. The preferred
method of preservation
is in sea salt, a method
that retains the flavor
and plumpness of
the bud. Capers make
a piquant addition
to any dish and
should be added just
before serving.

~ *Pizza Vongole* ~

CLAM PIZZA

When using a wood-burning oven, in which pizza cooks in 2 minutes or less, the raw clams are placed directly on the pizzas before baking. In a conventional oven, the clams are cooked first, as in the directions below.

3 tablespoons extra-virgin olive oil, plus oil for brushing

1/2 cup chopped onion

3 cloves garlic, sliced

1 cup dry white wine

1/4 cup minced fresh flat-leaf parsley

3 pounds small, fresh clams, scrubbed

Classic Pizza Dough (page 32) or Quick-Rise Pizza Dough (page 48)

6 cloves garlic, minced

1/4 cup salt-cured capers, rinsed and drained

In a large, heavy skillet over medium-high heat, heat the 3 tablespoons olive oil. Add the onion and sliced garlic and sauté until softened but not browned. Add the wine, parsley, and clams. Cover and cook over high heat, shaking pan occasionally, until all of the clams have opened, about 5 minutes. With a slotted spoon, remove the clams and set aside to cool. Discard any clams that have not opened. Strain the cooking liquid and reserve the cooked onion and garlic mixture.

When the clams are cool enough to handle, discard the shell halves without the meat. Trim away the valve and return the clam to the half shell. Spoon 1 teaspoon of the reserved onion mixture on top of each clam and set aside.

Preheat an oven to 500°F for at least 30 minutes with a pizza stone inside.

Pat, and then stretch each ball of dough to a thickness of 1/4 inch, leaving the outer edge, the *cornicione*, slightly thicker. Each round will be about 10 inches in diameter. Place each round on a flour-dusted pizza paddle. Brush each pizza with olive oil, leaving a 1/2-inch rim. Distribute the minced garlic evenly among the pizzas.

Slide the pizzas onto the pizza stone and bake for 4 to 5 minutes, or until the edges are golden brown. Remove from the oven, place the capers and cooked clams in their shells on the pizzas, and serve at once. *Makes six 10-inch pizzas; serves 6*

~ *Pizza Puttanesca di Don Salvatore* ~

PIZZA WITH OLIVES, ANCHOVIES, TOMATOES, AND CAPERS

This pizza has a real Mediterranean feeling, but warn your guests—the olives are not pitted!

Classic Pizza Dough (page 39) or Quick-Rise
Pizza Dough (page 48)
1 cup Pizza-Maker's Sauce (page 49)
10 ounces mozzarella di bufala, sliced very thin
1/4 cup coarsely grated Parmigiano-Reggiano cheese

1 cup unpitted Italian or Greek black olives
2 ounces salt-cured anchovy fillets, rinsed and drained
3 large tomatoes, cut into wedges
2 tablespoons salt-cured capers, rinsed and drained

Preheat an oven to 500°F for at least 30 minutes with a pizza stone inside.

Pat, and then stretch each ball of dough to a thickness of 1/4 inch, leaving the outer edge, the *cornicione*, slightly thicker. Each round will be about 10 inches in diameter. Place each round on a flour-dusted pizza paddle. Place some of the sauce in the center of each pizza, spreading to cover the surface but leaving a 1/2-inch rim. Divide the mozzarella evenly among the rounds. Distribute the Parmigiano-Reggiano evenly over the top of the mozzarella. Arrange the olives, anchovies, tomato, and capers randomly but evenly over the top of the cheeses.

Slide the pizzas onto the pizza stone and bake for 4 to 5 minutes, or until the edges are golden brown. Remove from the oven and serve at once. *Makes six 10-inch pizzas; serves 6*

~ Pizza Bianca da Di Matteo ~

WHITE PIZZA

This is the poor man's pizza, with only garlic and oil on top. It is one of my family's favorites. When we have eaten our fill of pizza with other toppings, I use the rest of the dough to make Pizza Bianca, then we take it in our lunch the next day.

6 tablespoons extra-virgin olive oil

3 cloves garlic, minced

1 teaspoon minced fresh rosemary

Sea salt to taste

Classic Pizza Dough (page 39) or Quick-Rise Pizza Dough (page 48)

Preheat an oven to 500°F for at least 30 minutes with a pizza stone inside.

In a small bowl, combine the olive oil, garlic, rosemary, and salt. Pat, and then stretch each ball of dough to a thickness of 1/4 inch, leaving the outer edge, the *cornicione*, slightly thicker. Each round will be about 10 inches in diameter. Place each round on a flour-dusted pizza paddle. Brush the center of each pizza with the garlic-olive oil, spreading to cover the surface, but leaving a 1/2-inch rim.

Slide the pizzas onto the pizza stone and bake for 4 to 5 minutes, or until the edges are golden brown. Serve at once. *Makes six 10-inch pizzas; serves 6*

~ *Pizza Fritto di Umberto* ~

FRIED PIZZA

This fried pizza is a delicious snack on a cold day. The oil should be hot so the pizza will cook quickly and not absorb too much oil.

Classic Pizza Dough (page 39) or Quick-Rise Pizza Dough (page 48)

6 tablespoons extra-virgin olive oil

3 cloves garlic, minced

Seed oil for frying

6 tablespoons grated Parmigiano-Reggiano cheese

6 tomatoes, peeled and coarsely chopped

12 fresh basil leaves

After the second rise of the dough, divide it into 12 pieces. Pat, then stretch each piece to a thickness of 1/4 inch and a diameter of about 5 inches.

In a small bowl, combine the olive oil and garlic and set aside.

In a large, heavy skillet, heat 2 inches of seed oil until very hot but not smoking. Fry each round of dough for 2 to 3 minutes on each side, or until the edges are golden brown. Drain on paper towels. While still hot, brush with the garlic-olive oil and sprinkle with the grated cheese. Top with tomatoes and basil and serve at once. *Makes twelve 5-inch pizzas; serves 6*

According to
"Smithsonian" magazine,
Americans eat 350 slices
of pizza every second,
constituting a thirty-billion-
dollar industry. Burton
Anderson, author of
"Treasures of the Italian
Table," calls American
pizza "born again,"
describing the New World
variety of thick and
thin crusts, unusual shapes,
and toppings that stretch
the imagination
to its limits.

~ Gigino's Pizza by the Meter ~

Another great pizza for parties, this pizza was made famous by Gigino's Pizzeria in Vico Equense, a community just outside Naples. The dough can be made in two half-batches. And if your oven and pizza stone are not large enough to handle a yard-long pizza, make it in three components and join them after cooking.

5 packages active dry yeast
1-1/2 quarts lukewarm or warm water (105° to 115°F)
5 pounds unbleached all-purpose flour (25 to 30 cups)
6 tablespoons sea salt
4 cups Pizza-Maker's Sauce (page 49)

1 pound fior di latte (cow's milk) mozzarella cheese,
sliced 1/4 inch thick
8 ounces salami, sliced thin
12 ounces oil-marinated artichoke hearts, quartered
1 cup Italian or Greek black olives
2 zucchini, sliced 1/4 inch thick

In the bowl of a heavy-duty mixer fitted with a dough hook, stir the yeast in the warm water to dissolve. Add 1 cup of the flour and the salt and mix well. Continue kneading and adding the flour 1 cup at a time until the dough is smooth and not sticky, about 10 minutes.

Shape the dough into a ball and put in a lightly oiled container. Turn the dough to cover it with oil. Cover with plastic wrap and let rise in a warm, draft-free place (75°F) for 1 hour, or until doubled in volume.

Punch the dough down and transfer it to a lightly floured work surface. Flatten the dough into a rectangle about 4 inches by 18 inches. Cover with a towel and let rise for 45 minutes, or until doubled.

Preheat an oven to 500°F for at least 30 minutes with a pizza stone inside.

Stretch the dough to a thickness of 1/4 inch, shaping it into a rectangle about 8 inches by 36 inches (or 3 rectangles, each 8 by 12 inches). Place it on a flour-dusted pizza paddle to assemble. Spread a thin layer of the sauce over the pizza, leaving 1/2-inch rim. Top with a layer of *fior di latte* (cow's milk) cheese. Alternate the topping ingredients (salami, artichoke hearts, olives, and zucchini) in 4-inch bands, then slide the pizza onto the pizza stone. Bake for 4 to 5 minutes, or until the edges are golden brown. Remove from the oven, cut into 4-inch squares, and serve at once. *Makes one 8 by 36-inch pizza; serves 30*

Italian
Regional
Pizzas

~ Semolina Pizza Dough ~

The classic tender Neapolitan dough, achieved by adding pastry flour to all-purpose flour, has been copied and modified by pizzerie throughout Italy. One of the most popular modifications is the addition of semolina to the dough. Ground from hard wheat, semolina flour gives the crust a crisper texture. To further intensify the effect, flatten the dough with a rolling pin to knock out the air.

1 package active dry yeast
2 tablespoons granulated sugar
1-1/2 cups warm water (105° to 115°F)
3-1/2 cups unbleached all-purpose flour

1/2 cup semolina flour
1 tablespoon salt
3 tablespoons extra-virgin olive oil, plus
oil for brushing

Dissolve the yeast and sugar in 1/2 cup of the warm water.

In the bowl of a heavy-duty mixer fitted with a dough hook, combine the all-purpose flour, semolina flour, and salt. Add the yeast mixture and 3 tablespoons oil, then gradually add the remaining water. Knead for 10 minutes, or until the dough is smooth and elastic.

On a lightly floured work surface, knead the dough into a ball. Put the dough in a lightly oiled bowl, turn to coat the dough, cover with plastic wrap, and let rise in a warm, draft-free (75°F) place for 30 minutes, or until doubled.

Punch the dough down and divide it into 6 pieces. Form the pieces into balls, place on a floured work surface, cover with a towel, and let them rise for 45 minutes. *Makes enough dough for six 8-inch pizzas*

~ *Pizza con Aglio Arrostito* ~

ROASTED GARLIC PIZZA

This is a modern rendition of the Neapolitan Pizza Bianca. The original is topped with just olive oil and minced garlic.

This version goes one step further by roasting the garlic.

3 heads garlic

1/2 cup extra-virgin olive oil

Sea salt and freshly ground pepper to taste

1 teaspoon minced fresh rosemary

Semolina Pizza Dough (page 80)

Preheat an oven to 500°F for at least 30 minutes with a pizza stone inside.

Score around the middle of each head of garlic; do not cut into the cloves. Remove the top half of the papery skin, exposing the cloves. Place the heads in a small oiled roasting pan and pour the olive oil over them. Season with salt and pepper, cover with a lid or aluminum foil, and bake for 20 minutes, or until the cloves are soft. Remove from the oven and let cool while covered. When cool, squeeze the cloves of garlic into the olive oil remaining in the baking dish.

Pat, and then stretch each ball of dough to a thickness of 1/4 inch, leaving the outer edge, the *cornicione*, slightly thicker. Each round will be about 8 inches in diameter. Place each round on a flour-dusted pizza paddle. Brush each pizza with the garlic-olive oil, leaving a 1/2-inch rim. Sprinkle with the rosemary.

Slide the pizzas onto the pizza stone and bake for 4 to 5 minutes, or until the edges are golden brown. Serve at once. *Makes six 8-inch pizzas; serves 6*

~ *Pizza Siciliana* ~

SICILIAN PIZZA

Eggplant is Sicily's middle name, especially when it is combined with tomatoes, capers, and olives.
These ingredients make a wonderful filling for calzone as well.

1 pound eggplant, peeled and cut into 1-inch cubes
Salt for sprinkling, plus salt to taste
3 tablespoons extra-virgin olive oil
2 cloves garlic, minced
14 ounces fresh Roma (plum) tomatoes, chopped, or 14 ounces
canned tomatoes, passed through a food mill
1/4 cup Italian or Greek black olives, pitted

1/4 teaspoon dried oregano
2 tablespoons salt cured capers, rinsed and drained
Freshly ground pepper to taste
Classic Pizza Dough (page 39) or Quick-Rise
Pizza Dough (page 48)
6 ounces fior di latte (cow's milk) mozzarella,
sliced very thin

On a baking sheet, spread the eggplant out in one layer. Sprinkle the eggplant with salt and weight it with another baking sheet for about 1 hour. Rinse and drain the eggplant on paper towels.

In a large skillet over medium heat, heat the olive oil. Add the eggplant and garlic and cook, stirring frequently, 5 to 6 minutes. Add the tomatoes, olives, oregano, and capers and cook until thickened, about 10 minutes. Season with salt and pepper and set aside.

Preheat an oven to 500°F for at least 30 minutes with a pizza stone inside.

Pat, and then stretch each ball of dough to a thickness of 1/4 inch, leaving the outer edge, the *cornicione*, slightly thicker. Each round will be about 10 inches in diameter. Place each round on a flour-dusted pizza paddle. Place some of the eggplant mixture in the center of each pizza, spreading to cover the surface but leaving a 1/2-inch rim. Divide the mozzarella evenly among the rounds.

Slide the pizzas onto the pizza stone and bake for 4 to 5 minutes, or until the edges are golden brown. Remove from the oven and serve at once. *Makes six 10-inch pizzas; serves 6*

~ Pizza ai Tre Pomodori ~

THREE-TOMATO PIZZA

*This summer pizza utilizes three layers of tomato essence: canned Italian tomatoes, fresh cherry tomatoes,
and flavor-intense sun-dried tomatoes.*

Semolina Pizza Dough (page 80)
1-1/2 cups (12 ounces) canned Italian tomatoes,
drained and passed through a food mill or pureed
in a blender or food processor
1 tablespoon minced fresh oregano
3 cloves garlic, minced

6 ounces provolone cheese, thinly sliced
1-1/2 cups (8 ounces) yellow cherry tomatoes, halved
3/4 cup (6 ounces) oil-packed sun-dried tomatoes,
drained and julienned
2 cups (8 ounces) Italian or Greek black olives, pitted
Extra-virgin olive oil for drizzling

Preheat an oven to 500°F for at least 30 minutes with a pizza stone inside.

Pat, and then stretch each ball of dough to a thickness of 1/4 inch, leaving the outer edge, the *cornicione*, slightly thicker. Each round will be about 8 inches in diameter. Place each round on a flour-dusted pizza paddle. Place some of the tomato puree in the center of each pizza, spreading to cover the surface but leaving a 1/2-inch rim. Sprinkle with the oregano and garlic. Divide the provolone evenly among the rounds. Distribute the cherry tomatoes, sun-dried tomatoes, and olives evenly over the cheese. Drizzle with olive oil.

Slide the pizzas onto the pizza stone. Bake for 4 to 5 minutes, or until the edges are golden brown. Remove from the oven and serve at once. *Makes six 8-inch pizzas; serves 6*

~ *Pizza Romana* ~

ROMAN PIZZA

Outside of Naples, pizza Napoletana is a pizza topped with tomatoes, cheese, and anchovies.
But in Naples, the same pizza is called Pizza Romana.

Classic Pizza Dough (page 39) or Quick-Rise
Pizza Dough (page 48)
8 ounces fresh San Marzano or Roma (plum) tomatoes,
chopped, or 8 ounces canned Italian tomatoes passed through
a food mill or pureed in a blender or food processor

12 ounces mozzarella di bufala, cut into 1/4-inch-thick slices
1/4 cup grated Parmigiano-Reggiano cheese
Sea salt to taste
18 salt-cured anchovy fillets, rinsed and drained
Extra-virgin olive oil for drizzling

Preheat an oven to 500°F for at least 30 minutes with a pizza stone inside.

Pat, and then stretch each ball of dough to a thickness of 1/4 inch, leaving the outer edge, the *cornicione*, slightly thicker. Each round will be about 10 inches in diameter. Place each round on a flour-dusted pizza paddle.

Place some tomato puree in the center of each dough round, and with a circular motion, spread it uniformly over the round, leaving a 1/2-inch rim.

Distribute the mozzarella evenly over the surface of the tomato. Sprinkle each round with Parmigiano-Reggiano and salt, and top with 2 or 3 fillets of anchovy. Drizzle olive oil in a spiral motion from the center to the outer edge of each pizza.

Slide the pizzas onto the pizza stone and bake for 1 to 1-1/2 minutes, or until the edges are golden brown. Remove from the oven and serve at once. *Makes six 10-inch pizzas; serves 6*

~ *Pizza Pugliese* ~

PUGLIESE PIZZA

Puglia, the heel of Italy's boot, has a long coastline. This simple summer pizza emphasizes anchovies,
but could easily accommodate some fresh catch.

Classic Pizza Dough (page 39) or Quick-Rise
Pizza Dough (page 48)
1 cup Pizza-Maker's Sauce (page 49)
6 ounces provolone cheese, thinly sliced

2 cups (8 ounces) Italian or Greek black olives, pitted
2 ounces salt-cured anchovy fillets, rinsed and drained
3 large tomatoes, sliced 1/2 inch thick

Preheat an oven to 500°F for at least 30 minutes with a pizza stone inside.

Pat, and then stretch each ball of dough to a thickness of 1/4 inch, leaving the outer edge, the *cornicione*, slightly thicker. Each round will be about 10 inches in diameter. Place each round on a flour-dusted pizza paddle. Place some of the sauce in the center of each pizza, spreading to cover the surface but leaving a 1/2-inch rim. Divide the provolone evenly among the rounds. Arrange the olives, anchovies, and tomatoes randomly but evenly over the top.

Slide the pizzas onto the pizza stone and bake for 4 to 5 minutes, or until the edges are golden brown. Remove from the oven and serve at once. *Makes six 10-inch pizzas; serves 6*

"The most important thing is that the dough is good. Pizza is the dough. With the addition of the other ingredients, it becomes the mother, Margherita, or the father, marinara."
—Antonio Pace, President, Associazione Vera Pizza Napoletana

~ *Pizzette* ~

LITTLE PIZZAS

Pizzette are the perfect appetizer pizzas. For a party, offer them with a variety of toppings such as
julienned roasted red and yellow pepper and pine nuts, or smoked salmon and minced fresh dill added after cooking.

Classic Pizza Dough (page 39) or Quick-Rise
Pizza Dough (page 48), prepared through the first rise
2 teaspoons grated lemon zest
12 ounces fresh tuna, cut into 1-inch chunks
1 onion, thinly sliced

3 tablespoons extra-virgin olive oil, plus
more for drizzling
1/4 cup salt-cured capers, rinsed and drained
1 tablespoon minced fresh thyme leaves
1 tablespoon minced fresh flat-leaf parsley

Knead the lemon zest into the dough. Divide the dough into 12 pieces. Form each piece into a ball. Place on a lightly floured work surface, cover with a damp towel, and let rise for 2 to 4 hours (Classic Pizza Dough) or 45 minutes (Quick-Rise Pizza Dough), or until doubled in volume.

Preheat an oven to 500°F for at least 30 minutes with a pizza stone inside.

Pat, and then stretch each ball of dough to a thickness of 1/4 inch, leaving the outer edge, the *cornicione*, slightly thicker. Each round will be about 4 inches in diameter. Place each round on a flour-dusted pizza paddle. Lightly brush the rounds with olive oil. Divide the tuna and onion among the rounds.

Drizzle with the olive oil, slide the pizzas onto the pizza stone, and bake for 4 to 5 minutes, or until the edges are golden brown. Remove from the oven, sprinkle with the capers and fresh herbs, and serve at once. *Makes twelve 5-inch pizzette; serves 12*

~ Pizza di Scarola ~

ESCAROLE PIZZA

This pizza, traditionally served at Christmas, is an unusual combination of escarole, pine nuts, olives, and
raisins, sometimes accented with anchovies.

8 ounces escarole, julienned

3 tablespoons extra-virgin olive oil, plus

oil for drizzling

1/2 cup coarsely chopped onion

3 cloves garlic, minced

1/2 cup Italian or Greek black olives, pitted

1/4 cup raisins

1/4 cup pine nuts

Salt and freshly ground pepper to taste

Classic Pizza Dough (page 39) or Quick-Rise

Pizza Dough (page 48)

1/4 cup salt-cured capers, rinsed and drained

Preheat an oven to 500°F for 30 minutes to 1 hour with a pizza stone inside.

In a large pot of salted boiling water, blanch the escarole until softened, 3 to 4 minutes. Drain and immediately immerse in ice water. Drain and set aside.

In a skillet over medium-high heat, heat the 3 tablespoons olive oil. Sauté the onion until softened but not browned, 3 to 4 minutes. Add the garlic and blanched escarole and cook until tender, 4 to 5 minutes. Stir in the olives, raisins, and pine nuts. Season with salt and pepper and remove set aside to cool.

Pat, and then stretch each ball of dough to a thickness of 1/4 inch, leaving the outer edge, the *cornicione*, slightly thicker. Each round will be about 10 inches in diameter. Place each round on a flour-dusted pizza paddle. Divide the escarole mixture evenly among the 6 rounds, spreading to cover the surface but leaving a 1/2-inch rim. Drizzle with olive oil.

Slide the pizzas onto the pizza stone. Bake for 4 to 5 minutes, or until the edges are golden brown. Remove from the oven, sprinkle with the capers, and serve at once.

Makes six 10-inch pizzas; serves 6

~ Bonata ~

PIZZA ROLL

This rolled and sliced pizza is a distinctly southern dish. It can be filled with your choice of ingredients, but typically it has meat, greens, and cheese. It is lovely served as an appetizer or side dish.

3 tablespoons extra-virgin olive oil

1/2 cup diced onion

3 cups fresh spinach leaves

1/2 cup ricotta

Salt and freshly ground pepper to taste

Classic Pizza Dough (page 39) or Quick-Rise Pizza Dough (page 48), divided into 2 balls before the second rise

1 cup Pizza-Maker's Sauce (page 49)

8 ounces fior di latte (cow's milk) mozzarella cheese, sliced 1/4 inch thick

In a skillet over medium-high heat, heat the olive oil. Add the onion and sauté until softened, 3 to 4 minutes. Add the spinach leaves and cook until wilted, about 3 minutes. Stir in the ricotta and season with salt and pepper. Set aside.

Put each ball of dough into a separate lightly oiled bowl. Turn each ball of dough to coat it with oil. Cover with plastic wrap and let rise in a warm (75°F), draft-free place for 1 hour, or until doubled.

Punch the dough down and transfer one piece to a lightly floured work surface. Flatten the dough into a rectangle about 12 inches by 18 inches. Repeat with the second piece of dough. Cover each with a damp towel and let rise for 45 minutes, or until doubled.

Preheat an oven to 500°F for at least 30 minutes with a pizza stone inside.

Pat, then stretch each piece of dough to a thickness of 1/4 inch, keeping the rectangular shape. Place each piece on a flour-dusted pizza paddle. Spread a thin layer of the sauce over each pizza, leaving a 1/2-inch rim. Top with half of the spinach-ricotta mixture, then a layer of half of the cheese. Roll each piece up like a jelly roll from the 12-inch side, and slide it onto the pizza stone, seam-side down so it doesn't unroll. Bake for 4 to 5 minutes, or until the edges are golden brown. Remove from the oven, cut crosswise into 1/2-inch-thick slices, and serve at once. *Makes 2 pizza rolls; serves 6*

~ Pizza Ligure ~

LIGURIAN SHRIMP, ROASTED PEPPER, AND PESTO PIZZA

The area around Genoa is famous for pesto, that savory blend of basil, garlic, Parmigiano-Reggiano cheese, and extra-virgin olive oil. When combined with fresh shrimp from the Ligurian Sea and sweet roasted peppers, it delivers a colorful and tasty pizza topping.

2 cloves garlic

1 cup fresh basil leaves, packed

1/2 cup pine nuts, toasted

1/4 cup extra-virgin olive oil

3 tablespoons finely grated Parmigiano-Reggiano cheese

8 ounces medium shrimp, peeled, deveined, and butterflied

1 red bell pepper, roasted, peeled, and julienned

1 yellow bell pepper, roasted, peeled, and julienned

Classic Pizza Dough (page 39) or Quick-Rise Pizza Dough (page 48)

In a blender or food processor, puree the garlic. Add the basil and 1/4 cup of the pine nuts and process to a grainy texture. With the machine running, gradually add the oil to make a smooth sauce. Transfer to a large bowl and fold in the cheese by hand. Add the shrimp and roasted peppers and toss well. Cover and refrigerate for at least 1 hour.

Preheat an oven to 500°F for at least 30 minutes with a pizza stone inside.

Pat, and then stretch each ball of dough to a thickness of 1/4 inch, leaving the outer edge, the *cornicione*, slightly thicker. Each round will be about 10 inches in diameter. Place each round on a flour-dusted pizza paddle. Divide the shrimp mixture and pesto evenly among the rounds, spreading to cover the surface but leaving a 1/2-inch rim. Distribute the remaining 1/4 cup pine nuts evenly over the top of the shrimp mixture.

Slide the pizzas onto the pizza stone and bake for 4 to 5 minutes, or until the edges are golden brown. Remove from the oven and serve at once. *Makes six 10-inch pizzas; serves 6*

One of the favorite
Italian regional pizzas
is topped with onions,
herbs, black olives,
anchovies, and tomato.
This pizza changes
its name along the coast—
in Liguria it is known as
sardenaira; further north
it is called pizza di
ventimiglia or pisciadela.
The same dish in France
is called pissaladière.

The first documentation
of tomatoes in Italy
was a description by
Pietro Andrea Mattioli
in 1544. He called them
"pomi d'oro," golden
apples. At this time
they were used only as
an ornamental plant,
and most people thought
they were either toxic
or an aphrodisiac.
It wasn't until the
seventeenth century that
tomatoes found their
way into the kitchen.

~ Calzone Calabrese ~

CALABRIAN SUN-DRIED TOMATO CALZONE

If you drive through the southern region of Calabria in the summer, you are likely to see racks and racks of tomatoes air-drying.
This ancient means of conserving intensifies and condenses the flavor.

3 tablespoons extra-virgin olive oil, plus
2 tablespoons oil for brushing
1/2 cup diced onion
1 clove garlic, minced
2 ounces salami, cut into 1/4-inch dice
1 cup (8 ounces) ricotta

1/2 cup (4 ounces) oil-packed sun-dried tomatoes,
drained and coarsely chopped
1 tablespoon minced fresh flat-leaf parsley
Sea salt and freshly ground pepper to taste
Classic Pizza Dough (page 39) or Quick-Rise
Pizza Dough (page 48)

Preheat an oven to 500°F for at least 30 minutes with a pizza stone inside.

In a skillet over medium-high heat, heat the 3 tablespoons olive oil. Sauté the onion until the edges are golden brown, 4 to 5 minutes. Add the garlic and salami and cook until the garlic is softened, about 2 minutes. Remove from heat and stir in the ricotta, sun-dried tomatoes, and parsley. Mix well and season with salt and pepper. Set aside.

Pat, and then stretch each ball of dough to a thickness of 1/4 inch, leaving the outer edge, the *cornicione*, slightly thicker. Each round will be about 10 inches in diameter. Place each round on flour-dusted pizza paddle. Divide the filling evenly among the 6 rounds. Fold each round in half, pinching the edges to seal. Brush with the 2 tablespoons oil.

Slide the calzones onto the pizza stone. Bake for 4 to 5 minutes, or until golden brown. Remove from the oven and serve at once. *Makes 6 calzones; serves 6*

*Friggitorie, or fry shops,
maintain huge copper
vats of boiling oil to serve
up such delectable tidbits
as arancini, deep-fried
balls of rice; fritto misto,
a mix of battered seafood
and vegetables; and fried
pizza and calzone.
This tradition dates back
to the eighteenth century,
when street food was the
only food available to
throngs of peasants with
no kitchens. It is still
a vital business, surviving
alongside take-out
pizza stands, providing
sustenance to today's
crowds of students,
artists, and businessmen
on the go.*

~ Calzoni Fritti ~

FRIED CALZONES

Little fried snacks are common on the streets of Naples, usually right next to the take-away pizza.

3 tablespoons extra-virgin olive oil

1/2 cup diced onion

12 ounces fresh spinach, stemmed

1/2 cup ricotta cheese

3/4 cup grated Parmigiano-Reggiano cheese

1/2 cup crumbled Gorgonzola cheese

Sea salt and freshly ground pepper to taste

Classic Pizza Dough (page 39) or Quick-Rise

Pizza Dough (page 48)

Seed oil for frying

In a skillet over medium-high heat, heat the olive oil. Sauté the onion until the edges are golden, 4 to 5 minutes. Add the spinach, cover, and cook until the spinach is wilted, about 2 minutes. Remove from heat and let cool. Stir in the ricotta, Parmigiano-Reggiano, and Gorgonzola. Mix well and season with salt and pepper. Set aside.

Divide the dough into 12 pieces. Pat, then stretch each piece to a thickness of 1/4 inch and a diameter of about 5 inches. Divide the filling evenly among the rounds, leaving a 1/2-inch rim. Fold each round in half, rolling the bottom edge over the top and pinching to seal firmly.

In a skillet, heat 2 inches of oil for frying. Fry the calzone for 2 to 3 minutes on each side, or until the edges are golden brown. Drain on paper towels and serve at once.

Makes 12 small calzones; serves 6

~ *Calzoni Quattro Stagioni* ~

The cuisine of Italy is tied closely to the seasons. Try these 4 different filling recipes for calzoni for a seasonal treat.

Fall Filling

3 tablespoons extra-virgin olive oil, plus

2 tablespoons oil for brushing

1/2 cup diced onion

1 clove garlic, minced

6 ounces wild mushrooms, coarsely chopped

1 cup chopped black Italian or Greek olives

1 cup (8 ounces) ricotta cheese

1 tablespoon minced fresh flat-leaf parsley

Salt and freshly ground pepper to taste

Winter Filling

3 tablespoons extra-virgin olive oil, plus

2 tablespoons oil for brushing

1/2 cup diced onion

1 clove garlic, minced

8 ounces ground pork

1/2 cup Pizza-Maker's Sauce (page 49)

1 cup (8 ounces) ricotta cheese

1 tablespoon minced fresh flat-leaf parsley

Salt and freshly ground pepper to taste

Spring Filling

3 tablespoons extra-virgin olive oil, plus

2 tablespoons oil for brushing

1/2 cup diced onion

8 ounces thin asparagus, blanched and cut into 2-inch lengths

1 cup fresh peas

6 ounces carrots, blanched and cut into 1/8-inch-thick rounds

1 cup (8 ounces) ricotta cheese

1 tablespoon minced fresh flat-leaf parsley

1/2 teaspoon minced fresh mint

Salt and freshly ground pepper to taste

Summer Filling

3 tablespoons extra-virgin olive oil, plus

2 tablespoons oil for brushing

1/2 cup diced onion

1 clove garlic, minced

8 ounces zucchini, cut into 1/4-inch-thick slices and blanched

6 ripe tomatoes, peeled and coarsely chopped

6 ounces mozzarella di bufala, cubed

1 tablespoon minced fresh flat-leaf parsley

1 tablespoon minced fresh basil

Salt and freshly ground pepper to taste

Classic Pizza Dough (page 39) or Quick-Rise
Pizza Dough (page 48)

Fall Filling: In a skillet over medium-high heat, heat the 3 tablespoons olive oil. Sauté the onion until the edges are golden, 4 to 5 minutes. Add the garlic and cook until golden, about 2 minutes. Remove from the heat and stir in the ricotta. Mix well and season with parsley, salt, and pepper. Set aside.

Winter Filling: In a skillet over medium-high heat, heat the 3 tablespoons olive oil. Sauté the onion until the edges are golden, 4 to 5 minutes. Add the garlic and cook until golden, about 2 minutes. Add the ground pork and cook until lightly browned, 4 to 5 minutes. Add the sauce and continue to cook until slightly thickened, 5 to 7 minutes. Remove from heat and stir in the ricotta. Mix well and season with parsley, salt, and pepper. Set aside.

Spring Filling: In a skillet over medium-high heat, heat the 3 tablespoons olive oil. Sauté the onion until the edges are golden, 4 to 5 minutes. Remove from heat and stir in the asparagus, peas, carrots, and ricotta. Mix well and season with parsley, mint, salt, and pepper. Set aside.

Summer Filling: In a skillet over medium-high heat, heat the 3 tablespoons olive oil. Sauté the onion until the edges are golden, 4 to 5 minutes. Add the garlic and cook until golden, about 2 minutes. Remove from heat and stir in the tomatoes and mozzarella. Mix well and season with parsley, basil, salt, and pepper. Set aside.

To assemble the calzones: Preheat an oven to 500°F for 30 minutes to 1 hour with a pizza stone inside.

Pat, and then stretch each ball of dough to a thickness of 1/4 inch, leaving the outer edge, the *cornicione*, slightly thicker. Each round will be about 10 inches in diameter. Place each round on a flour-dusted pizza paddle. Divide the filling evenly among the 6 rounds, leaving a 1/2-inch rim. Fold each round in half, pinching the edges to seal. Brush with the remaining 2 tablespoons olive oil and slide the calzones onto the pizza stone. Bake for 4 to 5 minutes, or until the edges are golden brown. Remove from the oven and serve at once. *Makes 6 calzones; serves 6*

~ Pizza al Gorgonzola, Pera, e Nocciole ~

PIZZA WITH GORGONZOLA, PEAR, AND HAZELNUT

Gorgonzola, pear, and hazelnut are a heavenly combination. This pizza can be served as an appetizer, accompaniment to a green salad, or an interesting finish to a meal.

3 cups water

1 cup granulated sugar

3 firm pears, peeled, cored, and cut into

1/4-inch-thick lengthwise slices

Juice of 1 lemon

1 teaspoon grated lemon zest

Classic Pizza Dough (page 39) or Quick-Rise

Pizza Dough (page 48)

6 ounces Gorgonzola dolcelatte

1 cup hazelnuts, toasted, peeled, and coarsely chopped

In a large saucepan, bring the water to a boil. Add the sugar, stirring until dissolved. Add the pears, lemon juice, and lemon zest. Reduce heat to low and simmer until the pears are tender, about 10 to 12 minutes. Drain and let cool.

Preheat an oven to 500°F for at least 30 minutes with a pizza stone inside.

Pat, and then stretch each ball of dough to a thickness of 1/4 inch, leaving the outer edge, the *cornicione*, slightly thicker. Each round will be about 10 inches in diameter. Place each round on a flour-dusted pizza paddle. Distribute the pear slices evenly among the rounds, arranging them in concentric circles. Crumble the Gorgonzola over the top and sprinkle with the hazelnuts.

Carefully slide the pizzas onto the pizza stone and bake for 4 to 5 minutes, or until the edges are golden brown. Remove from the oven and serve at once. *Makes six 10-inch pizzas; serves 6*

~ *Piadina Romagnola* ~

GRIDDLED FLAT BREAD

*Piadine are flat breads from the region of Emilia-Romagna. They are usually sold, with a choice
of fillings, from take-out stands in the streets.*

2 cups unbleached all-purpose flour

1/2 teaspoon salt

1/2 teaspoon baking soda

3 tablespoons unsalted butter

1/2 cup warm water

3 tablespoons extra-virgin olive oil for cooking

1 cup (4 ounces) Parmigiano-Reggiano cheese shavings

(use a vegetable peeler)

8 thin slices prosciutto di Parma

1 teaspoon aged balsamic vinegar

In a large bowl, stir the flour, salt, and baking soda together. Using a pastry cutter, cut in the butter until the mixture resembled coarse meal. Add enough water to bring the dough together. On a lightly floured work surface, knead the dough for a few seconds, until smooth and not sticky.

Divide the dough into 8 equal pieces. On a lightly floured surface, roll each piece into a 6-inch round, about 1/8 inch thick.

Heat a heavy skillet over medium-high heat and brush it lightly with olive oil. Cook the dough rounds for about 1 minute on each side, or until lightly browned. Brush the skillet with more oil as needed, when cooking each round.

Sprinkle with Parmigiano-Reggiano and top with prosciutto and a drizzle of balsamic vinegar. Fold in half and eat at once. *Makes 8 pieces; serves 4*

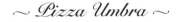

~ *Pizza Umbra* ~

UMBRIAN BLACK TRUFFLE AND POTATO PIZZA

*The green and mountainous region of Umbria is home to a renowned harvest
of black truffles with an aromatic, fruity flavor that defines the fall season. This pizza was inspired by
a delicious pairing with another underground vegetable of the season, potatoes.*

3 tablespoons extra-virgin olive oil, plus
more for drizzling
1/2 cup coarsely chopped onion
3 potatoes, peeled and sliced 1/4 inch thick
1/2 cup heavy cream
1 tablespoon minced fresh flat-leaf parsley

2 teaspoons minced fresh thyme
Salt and freshly ground pepper to taste
Classic Pizza Dough (page 39) or Quick-Rise
Pizza Dough (page 48)
12 ounces smoked mozzarella, sliced very thin
1 small black truffle

Preheat an oven to 500°F for at least 30 minutes with a pizza stone inside.

In a skillet over medium-high heat, heat the 3 tablespoons olive oil. Sauté the onion until softened but not browned, 3 to 4 minutes. Add the potatoes and cook until tender, 4 to 5 minutes. Stir in the cream, parsley, and thyme. Continue to cook until the cream is slightly thickened, 3 to 4 minutes longer. Season with salt and pepper and remove from heat to cool.

Pat, and then stretch each ball of dough to a thickness of 1/4 inch, leaving the outer edge, the *cornicione,* slightly thicker. Each round will be about 10 inches in diameter. Place each round on a flour-dusted pizza paddle. Divide the smoked mozzarella evenly among the 6 rounds, spreading to cover the surface but leaving a 1/2-inch rim. Distribute the potato mixture evenly over the top of the mozzarella. Drizzle with the olive oil.

Slide the pizzas onto the pizza stone and bake for 4 to 5 minutes, or until the edges are golden brown. Remove from the oven, shave the truffle on top, and serve at once.

Makes six 10-inch pizzas; serves 6

~ *Sfingione* ~

STUFFED PIZZA

Sfingione, or sfinciuni, is a popular Sicilian stuffed pizza. This version, with its simple and hearty ingredients, qualifies as "comfort food."

8 ounces eggplant, peeled and diced

Salt for sprinkling

3 tablespoons extra-virgin olive oil, plus oil for brushing

1/2 cup chopped onion

8 ounces ground pork

2 cloves garlic, minced

7 ounces fresh San Marzano or Roma (plum) tomatoes, chopped, or 7 ounces canned Italian tomatoes, drained, passed through a food mill or pureed in a blender or food processor

1/4 teaspoon dried oregano

Salt and freshly ground pepper to taste

Classic Pizza Dough (page 39) or Quick-Rise Pizza Dough (page 48)

On a baking sheet, spread the eggplant out into one layer. Sprinkle the eggplant with salt and weight it with another baking sheet for about 1 hour. Rinse and drain the eggplant on paper towels.

In a large skillet over medium heat, heat the 3 tablespoons olive oil. Add the onion and cook until softened but not browned, 2 to 3 minutes. Add the ground pork and cook until lightly browned, 4 to 5 minutes. Add the eggplant and garlic and cook, stirring frequently, 4 to 5 minutes. Add the tomatoes and oregano and cook until thickened, about 10 minutes. Season with salt and pepper to taste and set aside.

Preheat an oven to 500°F for at least 30 minutes with a pizza stone inside.

Pat, then stretch the balls of dough to a thickness of 1/4 inch and a diameter of about 10 inches. Place 3 rounds on a flour-dusted pizza paddle. Spread some of the filling in the center of each pizza, leaving a 1/2-inch rim. Top with another round of dough, pinching the edges to seal. With a sharp knife, make 3 slits in the top to vent the filling.

Brush with olive oil and slide the pizzas onto the pizza stone. Bake for 4 to 5 minutes, or until the edges are golden brown. Remove from the oven, cut in half, and serve at once. *Makes 3 stuffed pizzas; serves 6*

~ *Schiacciata* ~

TUSCAN FLAT BREAD

Schiacciata, also known as focaccia, has become universally popular, found from the northern provinces to the islands of the south. The toppings vary from region to region and season to season.

Sponge
1-1/2 cups unbleached all-purpose flour
1 cup warm or lukewarm water (80° to 90°F for compressed yeast, 105° to 115°F for dry yeast)
1 cake compressed fresh yeast or 1 package active dry yeast

1-1/2 cups warm or lukewarm water (80° to 90°F for compressed yeast, 105° to 115°F for dry yeast)
5 cups unbleached all-purpose flour
2 teaspoons sea salt
8 ounces sweet red seedless grapes
Extra-virgin olive oil for drizzling
2 tablespoons granulated sugar

To make the sponge: In the bowl of a heavy-duty mixer, combine the flour, 1 cup water, and yeast. Cover the bowl and let rise in a warm place for 3 hours.

Stir the 1-1/2 cups water, salt, and 1 cup of the flour into the sponge. Stir in the remaining flour 1 cup at a time until the dough is smooth and not sticky. On a lightly floured work surface, knead until smooth and elastic, about 10 minutes. Transfer the dough to a lightly oiled bowl. Turn the dough to coat it with oil. Cover with plastic wrap and let rise in a warm (75°F), draft-free place for 1 hour, or until doubled.

Turn the dough onto a lightly floured work surface and stretch into a rough circle 1 inch thick. Place on a flour-sprinkled pizza paddle. Dimple the surface of the dough with your fingertips, about 1/4 inch deep. Gently press the whole grapes on the top, distributing them evenly over the surface. Let rest for 30 minutes.

Preheat an oven to 425°F for 30 minutes to 1 hour with a baking stone inside.

Drizzle the dough with olive oil and sprinkle with the sugar. Bake until the edges are golden brown, about 30 minutes. Serve at once. *Makes 1 large focaccia; serves 6 to 8*

Pizzerie & Resources

Pizzerie in Naples

Ciro a Santa Brigida
(081) 23.37.71 or 552.4072
Via Santa Brigida, 71/74

Lombardi a Santa Chiara
(081) 552.0780
Via Benedetto Croce, 59

Di Matteo
(081) 45.52.62
Via Tribunali, 94

Da Michele (Pizzeria Condurro)
(081) 553.9204
Via Cesare Sersale, 1

Brandi
(081) 41.69.28
Salita Sant'Anna di Palazzo, 1

Capasso
(081) 45.64.21
Via Porta San Gennaro, 2–3

Antica Pizzeria Port'Alba
(081) 45.97.13
Via Port'Alba, 18

Umberto
(081) 41.85.55
Via Alabardieri, 30

Gorizia
(081) 578.2248
Via Bernini, 29

Don Salvatore
(081) 68.18.17
Via Mergellina, 4/a

Cantanapoli
(081) 764.6110
Via Chiatamone, 36

Trianon da Ciro
(081) 553.9426
Via Colletta, 46

Oven Supplies

Bravo Systems
7347 Atoll Avenue
Los Angeles, CA
(818) 982-7286 or (800) 333-2728
www.bravo-systems.com
Wood-burning ovens.

EarthStone Wood-Fire Ovens
1233 North Highland Avenue
Los Angeles, CA
(213) 962-5878 or (800) 840-4915
www.psservices.com/earthstone
Wood-burning ovens.

Mugnaini Imports
340 Aptos Ridge Circle
Watsonville, CA 95076
(408) 761-1767 or (888) 887-7206
Fax (408) 684-1501
www.mugnaini.com
Wood-burning ovens and clay tiles from Italy; classes for clients.

Renato Specialty Products
2734 West Kingsley Road, Suite L7
Garland, TX
(972) 864-8800 or (800) 876-9731
www.renatos.com
Wood-burning and gas brick ovens.

Wood Stone Corporation
530 West Front Street
Sumas, WA 98295
(800) 988-8103
Fax (360) 988-4302
www.woodstone-corp.com
Gas-fired stone-hearth ovens.

People's Woods
75 Mill Street
Cumberland, RI 02864
(800) 729-5800 or (401) 725-2700
Fax (401) 421 5120
Thirty-eight types of hardwood and charred wood.

Ingredient Resources

Balducci
424 Sixth Avenue
New York, NY
(212) 673-2600
Catalog (800) 225-3822
Anchovies in salt or oil.

Dean & Deluca Mail Order
(800) 221-7714
Fax (800) 781-4050
www.dean-deluca-catalog.com
Canned San Marzano tomatoes.

Food Matters
P.O. Box 14305
San Francisco, CA 94114
(510) 658-7388
Fax (510) 658-7404
Imported mozzarella di bufala.

Hirt's Greenhouse & Flowers
13867 Pearl Road
Strongsville, Ohio 44136
(800) 860-4478
e-mail: 73524.616@compuserve.com
San Marzano tomato seeds.

Manicaretti
5332 College Avenue, No. 200
Oakland, CA 94618
(800) 799-9830
Salt-cured capers.

Mozzarella Company
2944 Elm Street
Dallas, TX 75226
(800) 798-2954
Fax (214) 741-4076
www.mozzco.com
Fresh domestic mozzarella and fresh ricotta.

Todaro Brothers
555 Second Avenue
New York, NY 10016
(212) 679-7766
Fax (212) 689-1679
Canned San Marzano tomatoes, imported mozzarella di bufala, Italian Tipo 00 flour.

Vivande Porta Via
2125 Fillmore Street
San Francisco, CA 94115
(415) 346-4430
Fax (415) 346-2877
Canned San Marzano tomatoes.

For Further Reference

Anderson, Burton. *Treasures of the Italian Table.* New York: William Morrow, 1994.

Downie, David. "Where Pizza Was Born." *Saveur,* July/August 1995.

Field, Carol. *The Italian Baker.* New York: HarperCollins, 1985.

La Pizza Napoletana. Naples: GM Edizioni, 1995.

Ragaini, Robert. "Summer in a Can." *Saveur,* April 1998.

Romer, Elizabeth. *Italian Pizza and Hearthbreads.* New York: Clarkson Potter, 1987.

Schwartz, Arthur. *Naples at Table.* HarperCollins, 1998.

Index

Recipe Index

Acknowledgments

Pamela Sheldon Johns and Jennifer Barry Design would like to thank and acknowledge the following individuals and establishments for their help and support on this book project:

Kirsty Melville, Lorena Jones, Chelsea Vaughn, Amy Cleary, and Dennis Hayes of Ten Speed Press for their continued support and enthusiasm for great Italian food; Courtney Johns for his continued support and recipe tasting; Richard and Juliet Jung for travelling to Naples to photograph all the wonderful *pizzerie* that we may all now enjoy in this book. For this, in addition to Richard's lovely photography of the recipes, with the help of stylist Pouké, who makes every recipe look gorgeous and easy, we are most appreciative; Kristen Wurz, Tom Johnson, Leslie Barry, Carolyn Miller, Barbara King, Carol Hacker, and photographic assistant Ivy for their expert assistance in producing the book; Lucy De Fazio, Philippa Farrar, Linda Hale, Mari Bartoli, Ann Sprecher, Edna Sheldon and, Gioia Bartoli-Cardi, who offered support for this project in many ways; and Sur La Table, San Francisco, for props and tableware.